Rapid System Development

Using Structured Techniques and Relational Technology

Chris Gane

Prentice Hall
Englewood Cliffs, New Jersey 07632

Editorial/production supervision: Barbara Marttine
Cover design: Photo Plus Art
Graphics: Designations of New York City
Manufacturing buyer: Mary Ann Gloriande

ORACLE, SQL*FORMS and SQL*PLUS are all trademarks
of the ORACLE Corporation.

IBM PC is a trademark of
International Business Machines Corporation.

© 1989 by Rapid System Development Inc.
211 West 56th Street, Suite 36H
New York, New York 10019-4323

The publisher offers discounts on this book when ordered
in bulk quantities. For more information, write:

> Special Sales/College Marketing
> College Technical and Reference Division
> Prentice Hall
> Englewood Cliffs, New Jersey 07632

DISCLAIMER:
While all reasonable efforts have been made to supply complete and
accurate information, and to ensure that the procedures given in this
book function as described, the author and Rapid System Development Inc.
present this publication "as is" without warranty of any kind either
expressed or implied, including, but not limited to, the implied warranties
of merchantability or fitness for a particular purpose, and accept no
responsibility for its use, nor for any infringements of patents or other
rights of third parties which would result.

Printed in the United States of America

10 9 8 7 6 5 4 3 2 1

ISBN 0-13-753070-6

PRENTICE-HALL INTERNATIONAL (UK) LIMITED, London
PRENTICE-HALL OF AUSTRALIA PTY. LIMITED, Sydney
PRENTICE-HALL CANADA INC., Toronto
PRENTICE-HALL HISPANOAMERICANA, S.A., Mexico
PRENTICE-HALL OF INDIA PRIVATE LIMITED, New Delhi
PRENTICE-HALL OF JAPAN, INC., Tokyo
SIMON & SCHUSTER ASIA PTE. LTD., Singapore
EDITORA PRENTICE-HALL DO BRASIL, LTDA., Rio de Janeiro

ACKNOWLEDGMENTS:
My warmest thanks to Ron
Dougherty, Jay Marques, Gary
Rush, Trish Sarson, and Richard
Zultner for their careful reviews and
helpful suggestions, and to Keti
Szabo, who put it all together (again).

Contents

Introduction

The million-dollar question.

Suppose someone offered you $1,000,000 to develop a fairly simple on-line transaction processing system for them, say taking up to 100 sales orders a day at one location. The only catch is that after 60 days the contract price will go down by $50,000 for every extra day you take to deliver, and the price includes 5 years maintenance of the system (so the quality of the delivered code is important to you). Would you take the job, and if so, how would you go about it?

People give different answers to this question.

One answer goes along the lines of "I wouldn't take the contract. No non-trivial system can be developed and tested in 60 days (or 80 days, when the contract price is down to zero!)." This may or may not be true - certainly there will always be a certain number of time-consuming tasks to be carried out one after another - but it misses the point of the question.

The question can be stated, less vividly, as "If time is of the essence, rather than money or other resources, what is the best current management and technical approach to developing a system?"

A second answer is "I'd buy an application package."

If a package can be found quickly which meets the requirements of the business closely enough, or if it can be modified quickly enough, this can be the best solution. But the "if" is a big one, and raises two questions. First, how can the requirements be established surely and quickly? Second, once the requirements are known, how can a package that fits them be identified? The risks of failure are great, though the rewards can be sweet.

A third answer is "I'd evolve the system through prototyping."

As we shall see later in the book, the power of non-procedural languages means that a simple application, say involving capturing 20 data elements on one screen, querying them via a second screen, and generating five reports analyzing the captured data, can be produced in a matter of hours. Consequently, no great formality of analysis may be needed: a brief discussion with the users on Monday morning may be enough to enable the analyst/programmer to generate a prototype of the application by Tuesday noon. So what if it only handles 17 of the 20 data elements needed? As soon as the users see the prototype screens and reports, they will point out what is missing.

By the end of Wednesday, the whole application can be rewritten to incorporate them.

Such "evolutionary design" works best with simple applications that serve only one department. The difficulty with this approach is that as soon as the project grows over a certain size, beyond which the users and developers can no longer keep the whole system in their heads, such projects tend to suffer "creeping chaos" and can get into seemingly endless cycles of trial and redevelopment; what starts off as a small fast project can become a quicksand of complexity.

The answer given by this book to the "million-dollar question" has seven linked parts:

1. Establish the correct management structure for the project (discussed in Chapter 2).

2. Use an "impartial-leader group interview" approach for the definition of requirements (discussed in Chapter 3).

3. Develop a logical model of the system before making specific physical decisions (discussed in Chapters 4, 5, 6, 9, 10).

4. Use a relational DBMS with SQL (discussed in Chapters 7 and 8).

5. Use a full-featured non-procedural ("fourth-generation") language (discussed in Chapter 11).

6. Use controlled prototyping where relevant (discussed in Chapter 1).

7. Implement the system top-down (discussed in Chapter 1).

This combination of techniques represents best current practice for the rapid production of a quality system, with minimized risk of failure.

In Chapter 1, an overview of the seven-part answer is given, before discussing each topic in detail in the later chapters.

Chapter 1

An overview

1.1 Establishing the correct management structure

Every information systems project involves change. It may involve procedure changes such as using a CRT instead of filling in a form. It may involve organizational changes such as giving salesmen lap-top computers for automated proposal preparation, which will remove the need for proposal preparation staff in the branch offices, which will in turn reduce the power and control of the branch managers.

The changes implied by the system may provoke conflict, perhaps among middle management. For example, the marketing manager may want a new system to capture the customer's age, income bracket, favorite TV program and magazines; a requirement which the sales manager will bitterly oppose.

The more parts of the organization there are that will be impacted by the system, the greater the possibility for organizational change and conflict. By and large, people don't like to change, even if they need to for the good of the organization as a whole. So changes implied by a system may provoke resistance to that system. Overcoming that resistance and negotiating conflict takes time; that's one of the reasons why new system development can take so long. Further, it's hard for data processing people to overcome these resistances or resolve these conflicts since they neither know the business area well enough, nor do they have formal authority over the people involved. If friendly persuasion and sweet reason fails to get the sales manager and the marketing manager to agree, what then?

For these reasons, it has come to be recognized that a key to project success (and certainly to rapid development) is for there to be one senior business executive who takes responsibility for the success of the project. This senior user manager is the final authority on the scope of the project, the policies to be followed in developing the project, and on the organizational changes, if any, which the project implies or makes necessary. The manager who plays this role has come to be known as the "Executive Sponsor."

The Executive Sponsor convenes a definition and review group which should be made up of all of the managers whose areas will be impacted for well or for ill by the system being developed. This group is conventionally known as the "Steering Body." The Steering Body's primary responsibility is to reach consensus on the scope of the project, the objectives of the system, and the policy and organizational impact of the system.

The members of the Steering Body, in turn, are responsible for seeing that the system is implemented to the advantage of the business in their areas. This means that, for example, they are responsible for making available the best clerical or supervisory people to specify, in detail, what data should be held in the system and what the detailed procedures should be. These issues are discussed, in more detail, in the next chapter.

1.2   Accelerated   analysis: impartial-leader group interviews

In conventional information system development, the systems analyst interviews each user manager and business expert, one after another, making notes on the interviews, combining the notes into a requirements or feasibility document, and then reviewing this document with the people interviewed. Such serial interviewing necessarily takes up considerable calendar time. The larger the project, the more the interviews, the longer the time taken.

In recent years, the technique has evolved of carrying out the necessary interviews in a group, assembling all the relevant user representatives and the DP team in one room in a continuous workshop session which lasts a minimum of one day, typically three, sometimes five days. It seems important for the success of this technique that the session should be led by a person with no vested interest in the outcome of the project; somebody who is concerned to get a rapid consensus on a coherent set of requirements but is seen as having no particular interest in the specific choices which the group makes. The value of this approach - which has become known as Joint Application Design or JAD - was demonstrated initially by IBM and later by members of the GUIDE organization.

The techniques of these impartial-leader group interviews are discussed in Chapter 3. The main benefit of using them is that the requirements phase can be completed in dramatically less calendar time than with the traditional serial interviewing approach: reductions of 50% are commonly reported. (However, the group interview approach may not use fewer man-hours since more people are working concurrently.)

If conflicts are provoked by the project, they can be brought into the open and resolved rapidly. If they cannot be resolved in the session, such issues can be referred to the Executive Sponsor for resolution. The initial session on a project should be kicked off by the Executive Sponsor even if he/she cannot stay for the full session. This gives an opportunity for the middle managers present to see that the Executive Sponsor is serious about wanting the project to be a success, often a critical factor in database projects which necessarily involve the sharing of data and imply systems which cross organizational boundaries.

When well-run, these workshops go beyond the simple information gathering function of an interview; users participate in making decisions about the scope and nature of the system that is being developed for them, and come out with a feeling that "This is our system; the computer people are helping us build it."

1.3   Data/process analysis - logical modelling

When people think about an information system that doesn't exist yet, their ideas are usually pretty vague and general. This is not an accusation, but a fact of human psychology.

The purpose of logical modelling is to take these (necessarily) vague ideas that people have about requirements, and convert them into precise definitions as fast as possible. Part of the speed comes from having graphical techniques that enable one to put down the essence of a system without going through the trouble of actually physically implementing it as one might do, for example, in a prototype.

Logical modelling can be thought of as a seven-step process. Suppose the users say "We need a system that integrates sales, inventory control, and purchasing." What exactly does that mean?

Step 1 in logical modelling is to develop a system-wide data flow diagram to describe the underlying nature of what is going to go on in the sales, inventory control, and purchasing areas of the business. The simplicity of the data flow diagram comes from the fact that only four symbols need to be used to produce a picture of the underlying logical nature of any information system, at any desired level of detail.

This diagram shows CUSTOMERS (an external entity, something outside the system) sending in a stream of "Sales orders" along the data flow arrow.

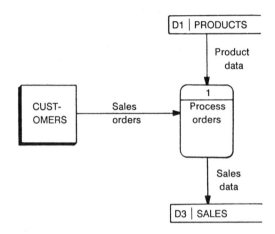

Process 1 "Process orders" handles those orders using information from the data store of PRODUCTS (the elongated rectangle, D1), and puts information about sales into the data store named D3: SALES.

The diagram on the opposite page shows the whole of the business area, depicted using only the same four symbols. For each sale, Process 1 updates the INVENTORY data store, D2, with the units sold. The data stored in D3 is used by Processes 2 and 3 to prepare bank deposit documents and send them to the bank and to prepare sales reports and send them to management. At some appropriate time (notice time is not shown on the data flow diagram), Process 4 extracts information about the inventory status of various products and combines it with information from D3 about their past sales, to determine whether a product needs to be reordered. If so, based on information in D4, which describes the prices and delivery times quoted by suppliers, Process 4 chooses the best supplier to order from.

Purchase orders are sent out to the external entity SUPPLIERS and information about each P.O. is stored in D5: POS_IN_PROGRESS. When (again at some later time), a shipment is received from a supplier, Process 5 is used to analyze it, extracting data from POS_IN_PROGRESS, to see whether what has been received is what was ordered, incrementing the inventory with the accepted amount, and storing the accepted quantities in the POS_IN_PROGRESS data store.

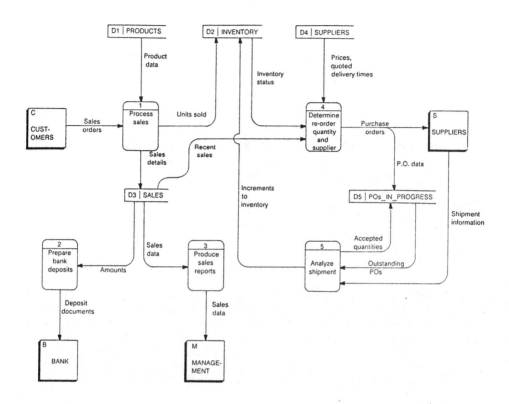

The techniques of data flow diagramming are discussed in detail in Chapter 4. For now, let us simply note the things which the data flow diagram (DFD) achieves:

1.   The DFD sets a boundary to the area of the system and the area of the business covered by the system.   Things which are represented by the external entity symbol (in this case, customers, the bank, managers, and suppliers) are, by definition, outside the system.

      Processes which are not shown on the DFD are not part of the project. For example, the diagram shows the receipt of shipments from suppliers but not the handling of invoices received from them.   This implies that "Accounts Payable" is outside the scope of the project.

2.   The DFD is non-technical. There is nothing shown on a DFD which is not easily understandable to business people who are familiar with the business area depicted, whether or not they know anything about computers.

3.   The DFD shows both the data stored in the system and the processes which transform that data. It shows the relationship between the data in the system and the processes in the system. (As we've noted, it doesn't show timing, but that's an important simplification.)

Step 2 in logical modelling is to derive a first-cut data model, that is to say, a list of the data elements which are going to be stored in each data store, as defined on the DFD.   This list should be drawn up from your own knowledge and the knowledge of users about what needs to be stored in order to describe a product, a supplier, a sale, and so on.

The list can be refined by looking at each input to the system, (such as "Sales orders" or "Shipments" in the diagram above), determining what data elements are represented by each input, looking at each output likewise, and then working from the outputs back to the data stores or from the inputs forward to the data stores.   For example, you might decide that for each product, you simply need to hold a code (to identify it), the product's name, and its price. This may be shown thus:

```
D1:    PRODUCTS
       Code
       Name
       Price
```

Often, you will discover that the data stores, as drafted, need "repeating groups" to be stored in them. In the case of D3: SALES, for example, for every sale there will be one salesperson and one date, but there may be multiple items included in each sale: the code for the product sold, the quantity, and a total value for the sale of that item. A repeating group is conventionally shown with an asterisk:

```
D3:    SALES
       Salesperson
       Date
       Item *
          Code
          Qty
          Total
```

6

The diagram below shows a repeating group in D4: SUPPLIERS as well as in D3: SALES:

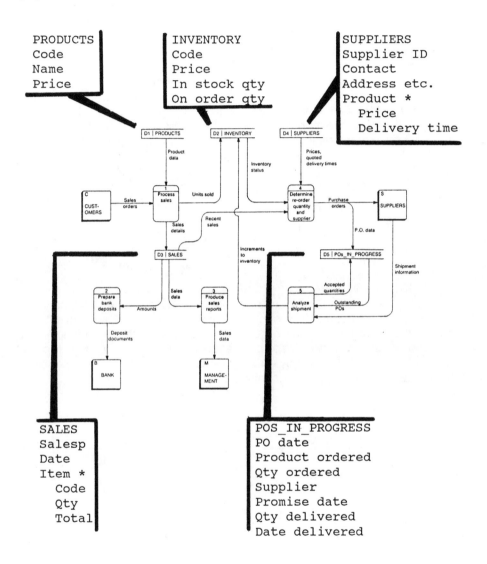

Unless the DFD is extremely large, it is very useful to produce a version which has the draft contents of the first-cut data model attached around the edge of the DFD with pointers, as shown above. (If you are not entirely happy with these data structures, relax; they will be modified later on.)

Step 3 in logical modelling is to see what entity-relationship analysis can tell us about the structure of the data to be stored in the system. We ask first, "What are the entities of interest about which data may need to be stored?" For this business, the answer might be CUSTOMERS, PRODUCTS, INVENTORY, SUPPLIERS, SALES, and PURCHASE_ORDERS. We create a diagram with a block for each of the entities we have identified. (It is conventional to state the entities as singular nouns, for example, CUSTOMER not CUSTOMERS.) Next we ask, looking at each pair of entities on the diagram, "What, if any, relationships exist between them?" For example, we know that one customer may be associated with many sales, but each sale can only be for one customer. This is conventionally shown by a line with an arrowhead against the "many" block, and a plain line at the "one" block, as shown here:

Taking PRODUCT and SALE, one product may be associated with many sales, but likewise, one sale may be for many products, at least one, possibly more. In this case, the relationship is shown by a line with an arrowhead on both ends. On the other hand, each product is associated with only one inventory record and each inventory record is associated with only one product. Consequently, they are joined by a simple line. Adding in all the relationships we can identify gives a diagram like this:

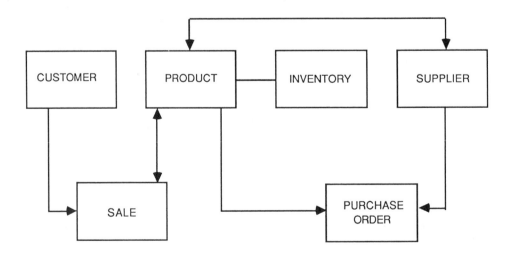

One of the most useful things about entity-relationship analysis is the knowledge that a many-to-many relationship can always be split into two one-to-many relationships by discovering the "intersection entity." Take, for example, the many-to-many relationship between products and sales:

This can be thought of as being made up of two one-to-many relationships, like this:

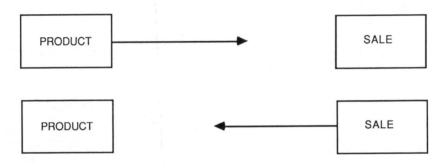

We put an "intersection" entity in between, with the "many" ends of the relationships ending on it:

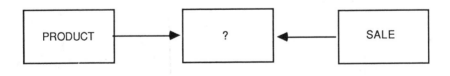

We then ask ourselves, "What is it that a single product may be associated with many of, and a single sale may be associated with many of, which expresses the relationship between products and sales?"

The answer, of course, is a sale item or sale item line, the instance of one particular product being sold as part of a potentially multi-product sale:

Taking a similar approach to the many-to-many relationship between products and suppliers, we can discover another entity, the "PRODUCT_SOURCE," which expresses the fact that any one supplier will supply any one product at a given price and a given quoted delivery time.

For each one-to-one relationship, we ask ourselves whether the two entities are truly separate, or can in fact be combined. In the case of products and inventories there would seem to be little case for having a separate table describing inventory.

So, putting all these considerations together, we would end up with a "resolved" entity-relationship diagram looking like this:

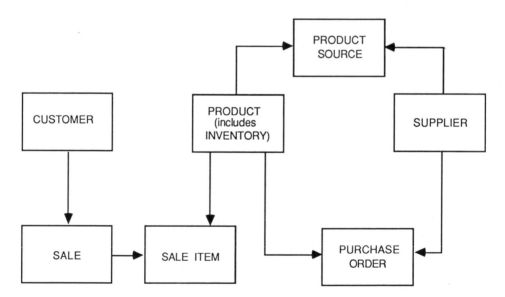

Note that the two entities that we discovered, SALE_ITEM and PRODUCT_SOURCE, correspond rather neatly to the repeating groups that we listed when we were doing our first-cut data model based on the DFD.

Entity-relationship analysis, which is dealt with in detail in Chapter 5, thus gives us a quick, very general, high-level look at the clusters of data involved in the system. Sometimes it helps us to discover entities which we have not detected when drawing a data flow diagram. Sometimes, however, it tends to include entities which are not actually needed. Take the case of CUSTOMERS. They are clearly entities of interest to the business, but from our definition of the DFD and from the nature of the business, which is a retail point-of-sale application, data will not need to be stored about them. The entity-relationship model tends to "model the world," to be more comprehensive than is needed.

Step 4 in logical modelling is to use all the information we have about the data so far to describe the data base as one made out of linked, two-dimensional tables. As described in Chapter 6, these tables should be "normalized," that's to say, made as simple as possible.

If you look at the example of the PRODUCTS table shown here, it has three columns: the code for each product, its name, and its price. In simplifying tables we care which column or combination of columns uniquely identifies each row in the table. In this case, obviously, it's the code. If you know the code of a product, you can pick out one and only one row of the table.

PRODUCTS

Code	Name	Price
T134	Spanner	11.99
T232	Wrench	13.55
T177	Pliers	8.19
P121	Paintbrush	3.85
H994	Bucket	6.55
H134	Garbage can	12.25

If you look at the table, PRODUCT-SOURCES, there is no one column which uniquely identifies a given row. Since any one supplier supplies more than one product, it's the combination of SUPPLIER-ID and PRODUCT that uniquely identifies a row:

PRODUCT_SOURCES

Supplr ID	Product	Price	Delivery
PER01	H134	6.95	10
HAV02	H134	6.50	14
PER01	T232	5.00	4
HAV02	T232	7.00	3
APP01	T232	7.00	4

The rules of normalization are dealt with, in detail, in Chapter 6. In essence, they say that in a properly simplified table, each non-key column should depend on the full key, and only on the key. Applying this to the data that we know we need to store (from the first-cut data model), gives us a series of tables like this:

```
PRODUCTS           INVENTORY                SUPPLIERS

K   Code           K   Code                 K   Supplr ID
    Name               In stock qty             Contact
    Price              On order qty             Address

SALES                                       PRODUCT_SOURCES

K   Sale no                                 K   Supplr ID
    Date                                    K   Product
    Salesperson                                 Price
                                                Delivery time

SALES_ITEMS              PURCHASE_ORDERS

K   Sale no              K   PO no
K   Product sold             Date
    Qty                      Product ordered
    Cost                     Supplr ID
                             Qty ordered
                             Promise date

                         DELIVERIES

                         K   PO no
                         K   Date delivered
                             Qty delivered
```

The K to the left of a data element signifies that it is the key identifier of the table, or is part of the key.

Confirming what we suspected as a result of entity-relationship analysis, we see that the PRODUCTS table and the INVENTORY table have identical keys, from which it follows that the two tables can be merged into one.

We see, however, something that entity-relationship analysis did not throw up: namely, that it's necessary to break the PURCHASE-ORDERS table into two, since there could be several deliveries covering the same purchase order. Typically, we would realize that we need to do this when we ask the critical normalization question "If you know the purchase order number which uniquely identifies each purchase order, do you automatically know the date delivered?" The answer, of course, is that you do not; therefore there must be a separate table with a row in it describing each delivery. (Even that is only adequate if there will never be more than one delivery on a given day.)

No later than this point (in fact, when we do the first-cut data model) we need to review the data elements that we specify so as to avoid the creation of synonyms (multiple names denoting the same thing) or homonyms (one name denoting multiple things).

Looking at the tables above, we can see that several synonyms have crept in. In PRODUCTS, the identifier is "Code," in SALES_ITEMS the same data element is named "Product sold," in the table PRODUCT_SOURCES it has the name "Product," and in PURCHASE_ORDERS it is called something different again.

Perhaps worse, there are homonyms. The data element "Price" in PRODUCTS is surely not the same as "Price" in PRODUCT_SOURCES; one name denotes the price which the product is sold at, the other the price at which we buy it. Unique names must be used to prevent this confusion.

Resolving these issues, and applying a consistent naming convention, would give us table contents like this:

PRODUCTS

K   PROD_CODE
    NAME
    SALE_PRICE
    IN_STOCK_QTY
    ON_ORDER_QTY

SALES

K   SALE_NO
    SALE_DATE
    SALESPERSON

SALES_ITEMS

K   SALE_NO
K   PROD_CODE
    QTY_SOLD
    ITEM_CHARGE

SUPPLIERS

K   SUP_ID
    CONTACT
    ADDRESS

PRODUCT_SOURCES

K   SUP_ID
K   PROD_CODE
    COST_PRICE
    QUOTED_DELY_TIME

PURCHASE_ORDERS

K   PO_NO
    PO_DATE
    PROD_CODE
    SUP_ID
    QTY_ORDERED
    PROMISE_DATE

DELIVERIES

K   PO_NO
K   DELY_DATE
    QTY_DELIVD

We can now redraft the DFD to reflect our more precise view of the system data as a result of entity-relationship analysis and normalization. This constitutes **Step 5**. As you can see, D2: INVENTORY has disappeared, having merged with D1.

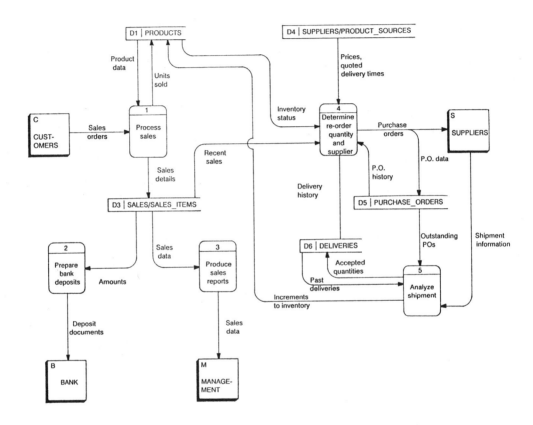

Two of the datastores, D3 and D4, are now renamed to reflect the fact that each contains two tables. Two or more tables are put into a single data store when they are usually accessed together. PURCHASE_ORDERS and DELIVERIES are given separate data stores since they are updated by different flows at different times.

For the most meaningful picture, we will include the normalized data model around the outside of the DFD, as shown on the next page:

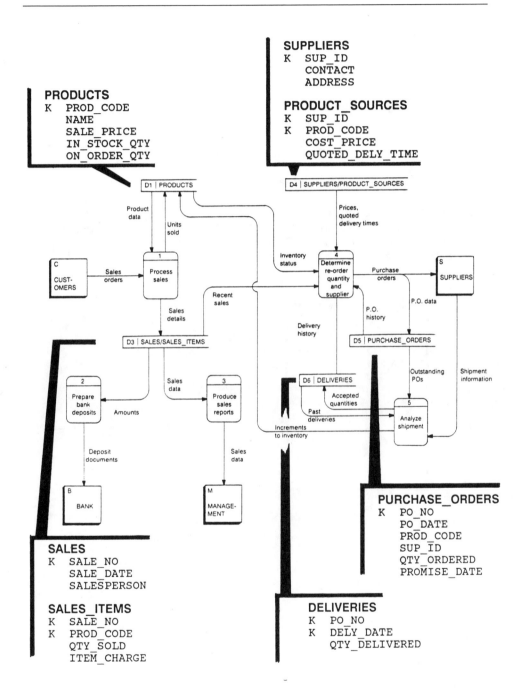

SUPPLIERS
K   SUP_ID
    CONTACT
    ADDRESS

PRODUCT_SOURCES
K   SUP_ID
K   PROD_CODE
    COST_PRICE
    QUOTED_DELY_TIME

PRODUCTS
K   PROD_CODE
    NAME
    SALE_PRICE
    IN_STOCK_QTY
    ON_ORDER_QTY

D1 | PRODUCTS

D4 | SUPPLIERS/PRODUCT_SOURCES

Product
data

Units
sold

Prices,
quoted
delivery times

Inventory
status

C

CUST-
OMERS

Sales
orders

1

Process
sales

4

Determine
re-order
quantity
and
supplier

Purchase
orders

S

SUPPLIERS

Recent
sales

P.O. data

Sales
details

P.O.
history

Delivery
history

D3 | SALES/SALES_ITEMS

D5 | PURCHASE_ORDERS

2

Prepare
bank
deposits

Sales
data

3

Produce
sales
reports

D6 | DELIVERIES

Outstanding
POs

Shipment
information

Amounts

Accepted
quantities

5

Analyze
shipment

Past
deliveries

Increments
to inventory

Deposit
documents

Sales
data

B

BANK

M

MANAGE-
MENT

PURCHASE_ORDERS
K   PO_NO
    PO_DATE
    PROD_CODE
    SUP_ID
    QTY_ORDERED
    PROMISE_DATE

SALES
K   SALE_NO
    SALE_DATE
    SALESPERSON

SALES_ITEMS
K   SALE_NO
K   PROD_CODE
    QTY_SOLD
    ITEM_CHARGE

DELIVERIES
K   PO_NO
K   DELY_DATE
    QTY_DELIVERED

Step 6 is to partition this logical model of process and data into "procedure-units," that's to say chunks of automated and/or manual procedures which can be executed (and therefore developed) as units. To do this we consider each input and output and ask for each one:

a)   When does it happen?

b)   How large an area of the dataflow diagram is involved in handling or producing it?

c)   Can that area be implemented as a single unit? And if not, why not?

To apply these considerations to the example we've been developing, take the input "Sales orders." When does this happen? All the time the business is open. How large an area of the DFD is involved in handling sales orders? It must be the area shown in the diagram below:

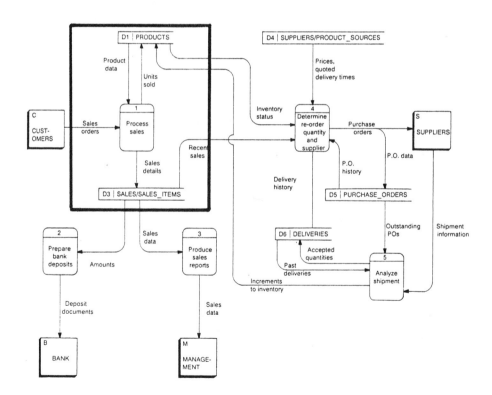

Can this area all be implemented as a unit? Yes, we envisage an on-line sales order-entry sub-system. The term "procedure-unit" is used rather than sub-system or program or module, since the implementation might consist of more than one program and/or catalogued procedure and/or manual procedure.

If we take the output PURCHASE_ORDERS, when does this happen? Let us suppose that purchase orders are generated daily at a time convenient to the Buying Manager. How large an area of the DFD is involved in producing purchase orders? Well, on the face of it, it must be Process 4 and the data stores which Process 4 accesses. Can that one process be implemented as a single chunk of software? No. What must happen, first of all, is that the inventory status of each product must be compared with the recent past sales of that product to see which products are in danger of running out of stock in the light of current and projected sales. That process will produce a list of candidates for reordering which the Buying Manager must review. The Buying Manager might decide that some products should not be reordered, even though their stock is running very low. For example, if the stock of Christmas trees is almost exhausted on the day after Christmas, that's a tribute to the Buying Manager's good judgment, rather than a reason to reorder; the computer may not know details like this, which is why totally automated reordering tends to be risky.

The human manager must thus decide which of the candidate products *should* be reordered, and will then need another chunk of software to look at the relevant suppliers and their offerings of price and delivery time, so as to decide which supplier should be used this time to provide each required product.

Further, while it is conceivable that a purchase order might be issued for each product as soon as the Buying Manager has decided on a supplier, it's not practical to do so. If there are, say, 100 products to be reordered from a total of 15 suppliers, the Buying Manager wants to make 15 phone calls to suppliers, ordering a group of products from each, not 100 phone calls. Therefore, once the supplier has been selected, the potential order must be held until some later time when the Buying Manager can call up each supplier and, with a display on the screen of the products to be ordered, get confirmation from each supplier of each product's price and its promised delivery time. The Buying Manager will then actually place the purchase order, possibly with later written confirmation.

Process 4 thus breaks down into three parts when we come to consider physical implementation, as shown in the diagram on the next page:

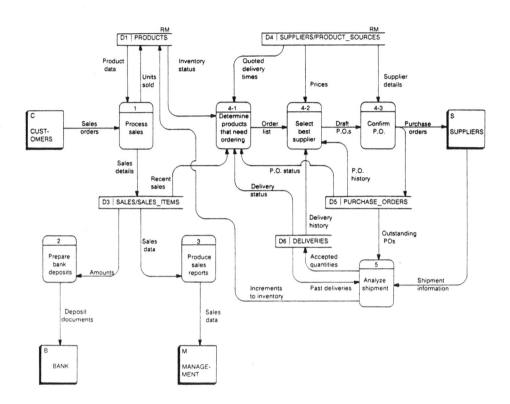

Process 4-1 ("Determine products that need ordering") draws on the inventory status of each product and compares it with the trend of recent sales drawn from D3, to see which products have a low inventory by comparison with their recent sales. Not only does it compute how many days worth of projected sales each product's inventory represents, it also looks at the unfulfilled purchase orders that have already been placed to see when we can realistically expect the delivery of new stocks, based on the supplier's quoted delivery time. The output of this process is a list of the products which are candidates for being reordered, together with all the sales and inventory information about each product.

Process 4-2 enables the Buying Manager to display any one of the candidate reorder products on the screen, to look at the various prices and delivery times quoted by the various suppliers of the product, to look at the actual history of delivery of purchase orders that have been placed with those suppliers in the past, and thus to decide on the cheapest supplier who can be trusted to deliver within an acceptable time, in the light of current inventory.

Process 4-3 allows the Buying Manager to display the details of a given supplier on the screen and to see all of the products which he has tentatively decided to order from that supplier as a result of Process 4-2. Then in the course of a single phone call, the Buying Manager can get the supplier's confirmation of their price and their quoted delivery time, and place a telephone purchase order to be confirmed in writing. Details of purchase orders actually placed are stored in the datastore D5: PURCHASE_ORDERS.

From this simple partitioned DFD, we can thus see that we need a total of nine procedure-units in order to implement the system (one for each of the 7 procedures shown on the diagram plus 2 to carry out routine maintenance of data stores D1 and D4, respectively.) As the table below shows, each of these can be listed with their timing and nature tabulated.

ID	DFD name	Type	When run	On-line/batch
		I = Triggered by input *T = Triggered by time* *M = Driven by management demand*		
1	Process orders	I	All the time business is open	O
2	Prepare bank deposits	T	Daily, in time for Bank cut-off	B
3	Sales reports	T/M	End of day, or as required	B
4-1	Determine products that need ordering	T	End of day	B
4-2	Select best supplier	M	On demand by Buying Manager	O
4-3	Confirm PO	M	"	O
5	Analyze shipment	I	When a delivery arrives at loading bay	O
6	Maintain PRODUCTS	M	On price change, new product, etc.	O
7	Maintain SUPPLIERS/ PRODUCT_SOURCES	I	When notified of change	O

Step 7 is to specify the details of each procedure-unit which will be required to implement the system. As we shall see in Chapter 10, a procedure-unit specification may involve:

1)   an extract from the system DFD showing where this procedure-unit fits into the rest of the system

2)   details of the tables accessed by the procedure-unit

3)   layouts for any screens and reports involved in the procedure-unit

4)   notes on the logic and procedures to be implemented, written in Structured English or some other unambiguous form.

The next two pages show an example of such a specification.

Once the nature of the procedure-unit is defined, an intelligent decision can be made as to whether it should be prototyped or implemented directly in the target language. Indeed the screen/report layouts may be developed by prototyping, as discussed in Section 1.6.

We should note that Steps 6 and 7 in this sequence are not strictly speaking logical modelling, since they deal with the conversion of the logical model into a physical model. They are included in this account because they form part of the natural flow of thought processes from the start of definition through physical design of the system.

Example of procedure-unit specification

PU 1. (Process orders)

General description:

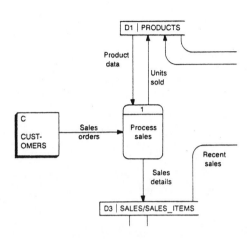

Allows salesperson to
capture customer orders
by entering product code,
and quantity purchased.
Displays product
description and current
price, and works out
transaction total.

When run: All the time business is open

Triggered by input. On line

Tables accessed:

PRODUCTS

K	PROD_CODE	Code to uniquely identify each product
	NAME	Product name as it will appear on reports
	SALE_PRICE	Price at which we sell product
	IN_STOCK_QTY	Quantity in stock after the last sale
	ON_ORDER_QTY	Quantity on order from all suppliers

SALES

K	SALE_NO	Number assigned by system to uniquely identify each sale
	SALE_DATE	Date sale is made
	SALESPERSON	3 letters to identify who made the sale

SALES_ITEMS

K	SALE_NO	
K	PROD_CODE	
	QTY_SOLD	Quantity of units of product in this item
	ITEM_CHARGE	Actual charge for this item

Screens/report layouts

```
== Handy Hardware Inc., 10000 Broadway, Erewhon City ==  Sale no: 100001
Salesperson: AAA         Wednesday 10 Sep 86  11:14 am       Tax rate % : 5
- - - - - - - - - - - - - - - - - - - - - - - - - - - - - - - - - - - -
Code  Item       Description      Price  Qty  $-cost     Tax   Item tot
H995  Bucket     24 quart         10.95   1   10.95     0.55     11.50
H134  Refuse bin Pedal opening    13.25   2   26.50     1.33     27.83
T232  Wrench     Adjustable       13.95   3   41.85     2.09     43.94




                                                        -----   -------
                                       Sale totals:     3.97     83.27
- - - - - - - - - - - - - - - - - - - - - - - - - - - - - - - - - - - -
How paid  (CAsh,AX,VI,MC): CA                  Cash tendered:   90.00
                                             Amount of change:    6.73

=== Thank you for shopping at Handy;  for delivery call 212/245-8870 ===
```

Processing notes:

Operator action	System action
Enter the PROD_CODE for a sale	Retrieve and display ITEM, DESCRIPTION and SALE_PRICE
Enter QTY_SOLD	Compute DOLLAR_COST (QTY_SOLD x SALE_PRICE) ITEM_TAX (DOLLAR_COST x TAX_RATE) ITEM_CHARGE(DOLLAR_COST + ITEM_TAX)
	When all items have been entered, compute GRAND_TOTAL
Enter HOW_PAID If cash, enter CASH_TENDERED	
	Compute CHANGE (CASH_TENDERED – GRAND_TOTAL) Print receipt for customer Store: SALE_NO PROD_CODE QTY_SOLD ITEM_CHARGE SALESPERSON SALE_DATE

1.4 Relational database management and SQL

Since the early '70s it has been known that, in principle, databases using only simple data structures are much more flexible (and therefore quicker and easier to create and change) than databases with more complex record structures (for example, hierarchical like IMS, or network like IDMS).

Codd's classic paper (Ref 1-1) laid down a model for a database which would be made out of 2-dimensional tables, the simplest data structures possible. Since this model was based on the mathematics of set-theory, in which a certain kind of table is referred to as a "relation," Codd described it as a "relational" database. "Relational" thus means simply "made out of tables."

One important feature of a relational database management system is that it should have an "active" data dictionary: this is another set of tables which holds the name, specification and location of each column in each table. This means that programs written using a relational DBMS don't have to contain data definitions; a program just "asks for what it wants, by name and table."

For example, if a table (named SALES) has been created in the database holding details of sales like this:

```
HOW_PAID AMOUNT
-------- ------
Cash       43.12
Amex      117.29
M/charge   27.00
Cash        5.19
VISA       32.50
Cash       11.25
   .          .
   .          .
   .          .
```

perhaps with 100 sales in all, then the one-statement program (in SQL, or Structured Query Language):

```
SELECT HOW_PAID, COUNT(*), SUM(AMOUNT)
    FROM SALES
        GROUP BY HOW_PAID;
```

will produce a report looking like this:

HOW_PAID	COUNT(*)	SUM(AMOUNT)
Amex	8	256.10
Cash	67	2232.60
M/charge	12	439.40
VISA	13	452.50

The SQL software will use the data dictionary to determine where the values for HOW_PAID and AMOUNT are stored, and will retrieve, summarize, and display them as shown. Furthermore, since the definition of the SALES table is held in the data dictionary and not in the program, the structure of the table can be changed later (for example, if another column is needed) without requiring any change to the programs which use it.

SQL (discussed in more detail in Chapter 7) has become the standard language for accessing relational databases. Compared with earlier languages like COBOL, it allows much faster programming for database queries (typical reports quote half the time or less), and much easier maintenance.

The SELECT statement above retrieved data from only one table, SALES. SQL also allows data in several tables to be combined (joined) to generate a report. Whenever a query involves a join of two or more tables, there is a possibility of slow response, because the read head of the disk drive may have to move to one table, read it, move to another table to read a matching row, move back to the original table, and so on, repeatedly.

Much ingenuity is being given to devising relational DBMS query optimizers that join tables as efficiently as possible. Faster disk drives make a difference. Of course, if enough main memory is available to hold the tables involved, the joining process takes very little time, since no movement of a disk head is needed at all. The issues involved in getting acceptable performance from relational DBMSs are discussed in Chapter 8.

1.5   Using non-procedural languages

What does "non-procedural mean?   What is a fourth-generation language?

In recent years, many attempts have been made to produce a language for application development which would be faster to write and easier to maintain than COBOL or PL/I.

Such a language should be less procedural than COBOL.   What does "less procedural" mean?   The "taxi-driver" analogy is useful in illustrating this point. If I get into a taxi in Manhattan, and say "Take me to Kennedy Airport," I am expressing *what* I want, but not *how* it is to be done (since there are many ways out of Manhattan).   If I say, "Go east on 56th Street, turn right on Park Avenue, then left on 36th Street to the Mid-town tunnel..." I am stating how I want the task to be accomplished in general terms (the COBOL level).   Though each instruction makes sense in terms of the goal, the full description of the task will take many more instructions than "Take me to Kennedy Airport."

If I say "Put your right foot on the footbrake, and move the gear lever into Drive. Look in the rear-view mirror, and if nothing is coming, pull out onto 56th Street. Drive along it at 20 mph until..." I am specifying how the task should be done in much greater detail again (the Assembly Language level).

If I were to specify the movement of each muscle in the driver's body at each moment of the trip, I would be giving a procedural specification at the machine-code level.   Procedurality is relative.

If the machine-code used to program the early computers with strings of 1's and 0's represents the first generation of computer languages, and assembly language represents the second generation, then languages like COBOL, PL/I, BASIC and C can be seen as representing the third generation.   By extension, the term "fourth generation language" (4GL) has been very loosely applied to languages (such as SQL and its supersets, NATURAL, MANTIS, FOCUS and NOMAD) which are less procedural than COBOL.

What would be the equivalent, in computer language terms, of "Take me to the airport?"

Any such language must provide in the fewest possible number of keystrokes or mouse-movements for:

▪   screen definition and editing of data entered via the screen

- computation and string manipulation

- retrieval from and update of the database (here, the SQL standard should be used)

- generation of printed reports/screen displays.

Not all so-called 4GLs provide all of these facilities, at least, not within the same set of statements which are interpreted or compiled in the same way. Most 4GLs are "clusters of sub-languages." For example, ORACLE provides one sub-language for screen-handling (SQL*FORMS) and another sub-language for database querying (SQL*PLUS).

In the view of this book, a "full-feature" 4GL should at least provide:

1.   a screen painting facility, which has access to a data dictionary, so that the user can point to the position on the screen where a field is to be placed, and name the field, whereupon the screen painter will extract its length and type from the data dictionary.

2.   the ability for the user to describe a screen-field through a standard questionnaire, which prompts the user to specify the position (if not already set through the screen-painter), the appearance (high-intensity, reverse video etc.), any default value, and so on.

3.   a default application-generator, which given the name of an existing table, will use built-in rules to create a screen layout for displaying the contents of that table, and automatically write a program for inserting, changing, deleting, and querying records in that table, from the screen. With such a "one-minute-programmer" default generator, once a table has been created in the database (so the names and data types of its columns are stored in the dictionary), the user can command the software to create a default application for that table.   The software will look at the column definitions and see how they can best be laid out on the screen. For example, if the table is small, so the column-widths with spaces between them add up to 80 or less, the application generator will lay out the fields across the screen with multiple rows on one screen, using the column names as prompts above each row. If the table is too large for this, the software will lay out the fields on the screen as best it can, and display only one record on each screen.   The software will generate data manipulation statements to take data entered on the screen and insert it in the table.   It will also create a Query-By-Example-like facility which allows the user to enter perhaps, CA in a state-code column on the screen, and then to press a "Query" function key which will cause retrieval statements to be generated retrieving all the records

records in the table which concern California. Once a record has been retrieved in this way, it may be updated by simply typing the new values in the appropriate fields, or it may be deleted by pressing a "Delete" function key.

While crude in appearance, such a default-generated program can be very useful for prototyping a simple one- or two-table application. An example is given in Chapter 11.

One valuable aspect of such a program is that there can be no bugs in it. Since the only input to the generation process is the table specification then, assuming that the specification is correct, the resulting executable code must be 100% correct, because it is machine generated.

4. an "autoloop/non-branching" application generator with SQL statements. This is a refinement of the default generator. It allows the user to control the exact position and nature of all screen fields (ideally, through the screen-painter and the questionnaire mentioned above), to write SQL statements specifying what should happen when each field is entered, and what should happen when a screen (or part of a screen) is complete. As with the default generator, provided the fields are specified correctly, and the SQL statements express the user's intentions, there can be no subtle or hidden bugs, since the executable code is otherwise untouched by hand. Some testing will be required.

This level of application generator is referred to as "autoloop/non-branching" since all loops required are set up by the software, and the flow of control cannot branch under program control: it simply starts at the top of the first screen, and proceeds field by field (unless the operator moves the cursor around the screen, or has a "Next Screen" key available).

5. an application generator with full IF-THEN-ELSE logic. This provides much more power to the programmer compared with the "autoloop/non-branching" level of generator. The programmer can control whether fields are skipped over, how control goes from screen to screen, and can write unlimited logic (just as in COBOL or PL/I). With this power, of course, come all the problems of debugging the multiple logic paths allowed by a procedural language.

6. a report generator using the same syntax as the application generator.

1.6 Controlled prototyping

The requirements specification techniques discussed in this chapter so far have all been static, in the sense that a map gives an unmoving static picture of an area. Also, until we got to looking at a (static) screen layout, we were drawing *abstract* pictures (data flow diagrams, entity-relationship diagrams and so on) which show the underlying nature of the system, but don't show anything that the users will ever see.

To a user, of course, the screens and reports and other inputs/outputs, *are* the system; what goes on "under the covers" is less real. Further, a screen dialogue is not static: it changes with each operator action, often in ways which are hard to describe and visualize from a paper layout. As Boar says "It is one thing to look at hand drawn screens and pretend there is motion but quite another to actually hit the enter key and watch the system happen before you." (Ref 1-2)

For this reason, it can be very valuable to create a prototype version of an interactive procedure-unit, which actually displays screens and accepts input, so that users can get direct experience of what it will be like to work with the system, when it is eventually delivered. If the users actually need to capture 20 data elements, and only 18 of these 20 were identified during data analysis, then working with the prototype will quickly identify the 2 that are missing.

Obviously, software (such as a screen-painter) must be available so that the prototype can be developed much more quickly and cheaply than the actual procedure-unit, or there would be no point in doing so. Different levels of richness of prototype can be developed.

Unfortunately, the speed with which a prototype can be produced has encouraged some developers to minimize the effort they put into defining scope, functions, and data before starting to develop a prototype. We can distinguish "discovery prototyping" from "refinement prototyping."

Discovery prototyping

In discovery prototyping, only the most informal analysis of requirements is done before the developer produces a prototype to reflect what he or she understands that the users want. The experience of using the prototype encourages the users to think more concretely about their needs, and the prototype is quickly revised several times as the users get more specific and detailed about their requirements.

When discovery prototyping is successful, it can be dramatic. Significant interactive systems can be delivered from scratch in a matter of weeks. However, the risk of failure is high. There are two dangers to contend with:

1.   If the size of the system that evolves becomes so large that the users and developers cannot hold all the functions and data in their heads, the project can get out of control. No-one can define the scope, or determine where the system boundary lies, or be sure how the parts of the system fit together.

2.   The project can get into a seemingly endless iteration of trial and revision, often because user and developer are led to concentrate on the physical details of the displays, rather than the essential business purpose.

Informal surveys suggest that the majority of discovery prototyping projects fail, for one of these two reasons.

Refinement prototyping

Refinement prototyping starts from the point where a data flow diagram of the system has been partitioned into procedure-units (which may be quite early in a project), and is most significant for those PUs where the user and analyst know that there will be a significant interactive dialogue, but cannot define easily with simple screen layouts how it is to function. Given a suitable software tool, a prototype of the dialogue can be produced, and refined until the dialogue is workable.

> "What prototyping does best is to uncover small design
> oversights, such as leaving the invoice number off an
> accounts payable screen. That works because the end
> user knows his job better than the programmer does."
>
> Bob Stahl, *Computerworld*, Feb 3, 1986

Refinement prototyping also helps resolve dialogue questions such as the value of a wide scope vs. a cluttered screen. For example, it may be desirable in a purchasing system to show on one screen all the details about a supplier, the products they offer, and their past delivery performance on each of those products. But to put all that data on one 80 X 24 screen would make it unreadable, so a compromise must be found. Which is best, a screen with summary information on the supplier together with a scrolling area for products and a separate screen for delivery performance on a chosen product, or 3 scrollable windows, or some other permutation? Often only testing with representative users can answer the question.

As a general rule, the developers should show appropriate users a meaningful working model at the earliest productive moment. Even refinement prototyping is liable to fall into an endless revision cycle, which is why it needs to be carefully controlled.

1.7 Top-down implementation

While top-down implementation (TDI) is not new, it remains a valuable technique for reducing the risks of delays and project failure; the larger the project, the more valuable TDI becomes. Essentially, TDI involves creating a skeleton of the system first, just enough to test the interfaces between the various parts of the system, *before* developing the detailed code for the system.

Bottom-up implementation

The reason for using TDI can be seen by considering the normal, or bottom-up approach. Typically a system is designed, and divided into sub-systems, each made up of a number of programs. Typically, also, each sub-system is programmed and tested by a different group, with the programming work divided among the people available. Each program will be coded and tested, first on its own, then as part of a sub-system test. Once each sub-system is working, they will all be linked together and tested as a system, prior to acceptance testing and cutover. If all interfaces between sub-systems have been correctly and unambiguously specified in the design, the system should function correctly. But that "If" is a very big "If."

All too often, the interface specification is ambiguous, and is interpreted differently by different groups. Or, the group responsible for one sub-system decides to change the nature of an interface, and does not communicate the change successfully to other groups. Since, with bottom-up implementation, these interface bugs will not be discovered until system testing, they can have serious effects on the project. An interface bug often requires considerable rework to fix: if a sub-system has been coded and tested based on wrong assumptions about an input interface, then in the worst case all the programs making up the sub-system will need to be changed and retested. And this unpredictable rework occurs towards the end of the project, when the users are expecting to start using the system very soon.

Top-down implementation

A project using TDI avoids this risk by testing sub-system interfaces at the beginning of coding, before a major investment is made, so that fixing an interface is quick and cheap.   The implementation must be planned as a series of versions, each testing all interfaces, successive versions handling more complex data and/or performing more functions.

Version 1, the skeleton, takes in some very simple input, usually specified as having no errors (so editing is trivial), stores the input in the database, and provides some very simple output(s), involving just enough code to create a kernel for each sub-system, and to exercise as many interfaces as are practical.

Version 2 handles more types of input, maybe with certain types of errors allowed, performs more functions, and provides more outputs (maybe correctly formatted).   It must be tested as a formal project deliverable to ensure that nothing in the new code has given rise to an interface bug.

The number of later versions depends on the project.   Each handles more data with more added functions, until all the system requirements are implemented. Though, of course, logic errors and specification problems are still found during testing, projects that use TDI rarely encounter problems with interfaces late in development.

Other benefits of TDI

As well as minimizing the risk of interface bugs,   TDI has several other advantages:

1.   Better control over conceptual integrity.

No matter which program in a system a user may be accessing, the user interface should be consistent.   The user should perceive that the system behaves in the same way, no matter which part of it is being used.   Function keys should be used for the same operation in all parts of the system, error messages should appear in the same position on all screens, similar fields should be formatted in similar ways wherever they appear, and so on.

In conventional development, these integrity issues are handled by laying down standards which all programmers should follow. Unfortunately, if the standards are unclear or incomplete, or if some programmers happen not to follow them for any reason, the finished system may lack conceptual integrity. When is this likely to be discovered? In a bottom-up implementation, the system is exercised as a whole at the end of development, and conceptual integrity problems are likely not to be noticed until then. By this time, of course, if it is discovered that the screens in one sub-system use 'Esc' to go back to the previous screen, and the screens in the rest of the sub-systems use 'F10' for the same operation, there may be no time or money left to make the necessary changes, and the users will have to live with the defect.

In TDI, such deviations from conceptual integrity are more likely to be caught in the exercise of early versions of the system, before they have been built into many programs, and while there is time and budget to recover. The repeated exercising of the whole system also helps to maintain conceptual integrity.

2.   Closer integration between software and training/documentation.

The people who are responsible for developing training materials and writing user documentation often have difficulty during bottom-up implementation, in finding out what the nature of the user interface will be. This can result in the training and manuals not being available until after it is really needed during implementation.

With TDI, the skeleton version must be accompanied by some simple training to enable representative users to exercise the software as well as a skeleton user's manual. The second version will require additional training and a more extensive manual. The human sub-system thus evolves in parallel with the software.

References

1-1   Codd, E. F.   *A relational model of data for large shared data banks*. Communications of the ACM, June 1970

1-2   Boar, B. H. *Application Prototyping.* New York: Wiley 1984

Chapter 2

Management structure issues

2.1   Problems with multi-departmental systems

We noted in Chapter 1 that the changes implied by a new information system may give rise to conflict and resistance, and that the larger the area of the organization which is affected by the system, the more serious this problem may be.

There are several sources of such resistance and conflict, including:

1.   **managers who perceive that they will have to pay more towards the cost of the system than they will receive in benefits.**   Often the cost is not financial, but is in terms of extra effort required and inconvenience inflicted on a manager's people.   The classic case is that of the integrated sales and marketing system which would require each salesperson to ask the customer's age, income, and favorite TV program; in other words to do work (and risk customer alienation) to capture data which would benefit the Marketing Department in selecting advertising media and designing direct mail campaigns. Each sale would need an additional four minutes on the phone to capture the marketing data, beyond the time needed to close the sale.

From the Sales Manager's point of view, why should his people do this work? The Sales Manager is paid on the basis of sales dollars, and gathering marketing information means that salespeople will make fewer sales per hour, which might make it difficult for them to reach their targets and depress their commissions.

Here we have a situation where the overall good of the business (to increase the sales per advertising dollar by spending the money more effectively) is in conflict with the objectives of a unit of the business, and contrary to the self-interest of the people in that unit. Naturally, some resistance may be expected, to say the least.

2.   people whose power may be diminished as a result of the system.
Current trends in computer/communications technology tend to reduce the
power of local and middle managers.   Put yourself in the position of a Branch
Manager of a company with a Head Office 2000 miles away.   You have a force
of salespeople who call on prospects and find out requirements.   They bring
these requirements back to your office where your staff work out price
quotations.   Once you have received and approved the quotation,   your
assistant calls up the factory to get a delivery time.   Once the client approves
the order,   you transmit it to Head Office and bill the client.   To a large extent,
you are running your own business,   effectively buying what you need from
Head Office and selling it to your client.

Now an on-line quotation and order entry system is proposed,   which will equip
each salesman with a lap-top computer.   The salesmen will enter details of the
client's requirements into the lap-top and then,   using the client's phone,   dial in
to Head Office,   transmit the details of the requirements,   and get a quotation,
complete with price and delivery time,   printed out for the client to sign right
there.   How do you,   as Branch Manager,   feel about this proposed system?
On the face of it,   it will do wonders for your competitiveness,   since your
salesmen will be able to produce quotes in 10 minutes,   instead of 10 days,   as
happens now.   On the other hand,   you will no longer need your staff,   and will
go from being a quasi-independent businessman to being a "wet-nurse for lap-
top carriers,"   since all important decisions will be taken at head office,   and
your job will be to hire,   train and support salesmen who will largely work for
Head Office,   not you.

It would not be surprising if you,   and your fellow Branch Managers,   used your
influence with upper management to point out the dangers of giving so much
control to salesmen,   conspired to confuse and frustrate the systems analysts
working on the requirement and used your political power to delay the project,
in the hopes that it would be cancelled if it went on long enough without
showing results.   It would also not be surprising if during system trials,   some
salesman was to commit to sell something for $2,400 with 10 days delivery,
instead of the correct $24,000 with 100 days delivery.   "There,"   you would say,
"that shows that you need an experienced manager on the spot to review these
quotes: you can't trust technology!"

Somewhat similar conflicts between the good of the organization as a whole
and a manager's self-interest,   arise with production management as well.
Where a shop-floor supervisor has operated with manual reporting of hours
worked and job progress,   and has prepared the status reports that go to upper
management himself,   it can be a threat to consider moving to an environment
where workers key in their activities to on-line shop-floor terminals.   In an
extreme case,   a supervisor may get a call from the Vice-President of Production
in Head Office 10 miles away,   asking "What are you doing about the high

inventory of semi-finished parts on #3 line?" when he isn't even aware yet that the problem exists. Being a middle manager in an on-line environment, where your boss, and your boss' boss, can look at their CRTs and see what's happening in your area up to a minute ago, can be "like being a goldfish in a bowl surrounded by hungry cats."

3. **people whose jobs will become harder or more boring, or will disappear**, as a result of the system. While good design of the human procedures which will be part of a new system implies that the system should be workable and interesting to use, all too often clerical workers have seen their jobs made worse by information systems.

If you are a worker processing supplier's invoices by hand, where verifying an invoice takes 2 minutes, and you are expected to do 25 invoices an hour, you have a feasible job. If now a system comes along which will require you to spend 3 minutes entering all the data on each invoice into a CRT for the computer to verify, and if you are *still* expected to do 25 invoices an hour, your job has been made impossible. You might be tempted to be careless, cut corners, and enter bad data, and then complain that the system gives wrong answers. Perhaps you would even get the system to overpay some suppliers, so that management will cancel use of it, and revert to the previous manual system you were comfortable with (blaming the MIS department for producing a poor system). Of course, your invoice workload should have been adjusted to 18 an hour, but nobody in MIS had the authority to make such a policy change.

By the same token, if you have spent the last 27 years assigning invoice numbers and sales codes, and hear through the grapevine that the new system is going to do this automatically, you may become a little worried about your future. Whose job is it to decide what you should do once the new system is installed? Not the systems analyst's. Whose job is it to reassure you that you will be needed in another capacity, and will get retrained? Not the systems analyst's.

This consideration brings us to the key issue: if specifying the system precipitates conflicts among middle management, or if policies or job descriptions or organizational boundaries need to be changed, who has the power to deal with the issue? The MIS team, even though they may be charged with acting as change agents, can only recommend and persuade. If the Sales Manager and the Marketing Manager cannot agree on whether the salesmen should capture demographic data, in spite of the DP Project Manager's best efforts to mediate between them, how can a decision be reached so that the project can proceed? If people need to be retrained or reassigned, who has the authority to see that this is done, and done effectively?

2.2 The correct management structure for the project

1. The Executive Sponsor

It is generally agreed that the larger a project, and the greater the number of organizational units impacted, the more critical it is that a senior business executive should take final responsibility for the success of the project. This role is usually referred to as that of "Executive Sponsor."

Who should be the Executive Sponsor?

The Executive Sponsor's primary role is to ensure that if conflicts arise, or organizational policy decisions need to be taken, the issue is handled quickly, in a way that will be accepted by all concerned. For this reason, **the most effective person as Executive Sponsor is the person who has formal authority over all business units impacted by the system.**

This is a hard saying, because it means that very senior executives need to get involved with projects which, up to now, they have seen as being far too detailed to be of concern to them.

Consider the organization shown on the opposite page. A project to develop a new system for supporting salespeople with improved sales analysis procedures would impact Branch Managers and the Manager of Sales Analysis. The VP of Sales is the executive with formal authority over all these business units, and is therefore the most effective person as Executive Sponsor.

But what about the project we mentioned before, which will get salesmen to capture market research data at the point of sale, and transmit order information directly to production planning? The managers of each area that is impacted report to different VPs. The only executive who has formal authority over all the areas impacted is the President. Can one seriously expect the President to be concerned, other than at a return-on-investment level, with an information systems project? More and more organizations (and their very senior executives) are coming to realize that, strange as it may seem, such involvement makes the difference between success or failure for a project which spans business units in the way that this one does.

Another way to look at the question is: if not the President, then who? If the VP of Sales is Executive Sponsor, the Marketing Department will not get the data they require, and the needs of production planning will be subordinated to those of sales. If the VP of Marketing is Executive Sponsor, the salespeople may resent the system, and refuse to capture the data needed anyhow, at the

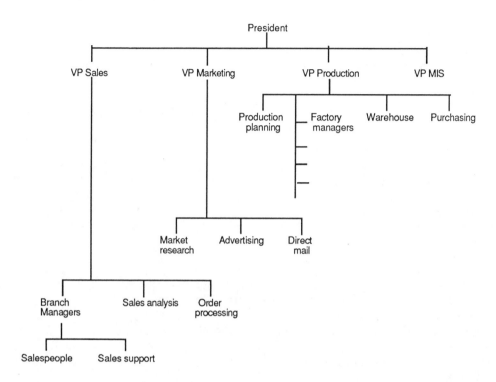

not-so-subtle urgings of their management. If the VP of Production is Executive Sponsor, the system will be biased towards the needs of production planning, and so on. If there is no Executive Sponsor, conflicts between the three areas will remain unresolved, and the project will probably be cancelled after months or years of fruitless analysis.

Reactions from the candidate Executive Sponsor

The President, in this case, may say, "There's no need for me to be involved: I'm sure the three VPs will work together for the good of the company, and sort any disagreements out amongst themselves."   One often notices an element of self-deception in top management's view of the differences and power struggles among their subordinates.   To this one might say "If the three VPs will reach a consensus, then the Executive Sponsor will not have to spend any time on the project, other than to give it his support, so your assuming the role should present no difficulty."

The President may turn to the VP of MIS and attempt to delegate the responsibilities of Executive Sponsor to him. After all, developing systems is what the VP of MIS was hired to do. If this happens, the VP of MIS should confirm with the President that he will be upheld in any business decision that he, the VP of MIS, may need to take. He may say, for example, "If the best thing for the organization is to insist that salespeople collect market research data (over the objections of the VP of Sales), and to reorganize production planning to make customized products (instead of the batch runs that the VP of Production wants), may I be assured of your support in whatever decision I take?" To this the President can either say "Yes," "No," or "It depends."

If the President says "Yes," the VP of MIS may then say "Would you please make the position clear to the other VPs," and "May I come to you with any issues where I'm not clear what the policy should be?" If the President concurs, he has effectively assumed the role of "real" Executive Sponsor for the project, with the VP of MIS as his mouthpiece, which though not ideal, may be workable.

If the President says "No" or "It depends" to the question of support, then the VP of MIS should point out to him the risk of failure involved in investing in a project without an effective Executive Sponsor, and suggest the project be delayed until the President *can* be the Executive Sponsor. Some organizations, after bitter experience, have settled on a policy of not undertaking any information systems project for which an effective Executive Sponsor is not available.

In some organizations, the management climate is one where top management is weak and the Vice-Presidents operate as almost independent "barons" with little consensus decision making among them. Whatever the virtues of such a climate may be, it poses severe difficulties for the development of any integrated database systems. Indeed, it may be that some organizations will *never* develop integrated databases: the management structure will not permit them to do so. Even if the management structure is sound, the best candidate for Executive Sponsor may be reluctant to undertake the responsibility because its non-technical nature and the very limited time commitment is not made clear enough. After all, if you were working 12-hour days as Chief Executive Officer of a growing corporation, worrying about new product development, marketing policy, government relations, management team building, production quality, international expansion, and the rest, you would have to be ruthless about taking on any open-ended responsibility, especially one in an area where you were not sure of your competence, and which you believed was properly the job of a subordinate. You would want to have a reasoned case made to you. The specimen memo opposite lays out the skeleton of such a case.

Specimen memo to selected Executive Sponsor.

Dear Senior Executive:

As you may know we are in the early stages of planning the integrated X information systems project, which you and your colleagues on the MIS Planning Committee have identified as being important in supporting the growth of our business over the next few years.

This system will impact Department P, Department Q and Department R, and as in all cases where a shared data base is introduced, may require some changes in the organization and day-to-day procedures in those departments. For instance, it seems likely that ... *(mention some possible changes)*.

Experience shows that where such organizational impacts are involved, there may be difficulty in getting quick agreement and commitment to change from all the managers involved, unless the executive with formal authority over all the impacted areas acts as the driving force behind the project.

Since you are the only person with authority over Departments P, Q and R, I am requesting that you play the role of Executive Sponsor for the X information system; this means that you would have the final say in the scope and objectives of the system, and would decide any policy issues raised by the implementation of the system. The specific time commitment involved, based on past experience, would be:

a) 2 hours to be briefed on the project and to give initial direction, including nomination of those managers who should be on the project's Steering Body.

b) 1 hour to kick-off the project strategy workshop.

c) availability through the life of the project to resolve any issues that cannot be handled by consensus among Steering Body members.

Where an executive of your seniority is seen to be behind a project such as X, many costly delays and problems are avoided, and the chances of defining and installing a system which truly serves the needs of the business are much enhanced.

Chief Information Officer

2. · The Steering Body

As the specimen memo mentions, one of the Executive Sponsor's responsibilities is to nominate the members of the Steering Body, who will set the scope and objectives of the project. The Steering Body should include the managers of all the business units affected, for well or for ill, by the proposed system. That is to say, it should include not only those who want the system, but also those who may offer resistance to it. The reason for this is that if resistances and conflicts are not brought into the open and resolved during Steering Body meetings, they will lie dormant while the project budget is spent, only to surface when the system is being installed, often to cause expensive failure.

Another reason why the Executive Sponsor should be the person having formal authority over all impacted areas is that he is in the best position to know who should serve on the Steering Body, and the person whose invitations to do so are most likely to be accepted. One way for a manager to express resistance to a project is to send a junior deputy without decision-making powers to attend the meetings. If the Steering Body definition and review meetings are called by the President, the VP of Production is more likely to attend than if he is requested to do so by a systems analyst from MIS.

Where a project will affect a number of similar business units, the Steering Body should include a representative manager of such a unit, who has the respect of all his fellow unit managers. So in the case of the project which will integrate sales, marketing and production planning, the Steering Body should be composed of:

> VP   Sales
> A Branch Manager (chosen as above)
> Manager, Sales Analysis
> Manager, Order Processing
> VP   Marketing
> Manager, Market Research
> VP   Production
> Manager, Production Planning

As well as setting objectives and reviewing the requirements definition of the project, the members of the Steering Body should take responsibility for the successful implementation of the system in their areas. No matter how well the software may be written, the people who will use the terminals and reports must be made available for training at the proper time. If procedures and job descriptions need to be changed, that must be done effectively. If clerical people need to spend time converting data from the old system to the new, before the new system can be used live, then their time must be made available. There are many such actions needed to make a success of an information system, so that it delivers positive results in the business; if the Steering Body members are chosen and briefed correctly, these things will be done well and on time.

This issue shows up the difference between the objectives of the information system, and the business objectives of the project. The system objectives can only be in terms of capturing, storing, and delivering data faster, more accurately, more comprehensively, or more useably. The business objectives, on the other hand, are in terms of increased revenue, avoided cost, or improved service to clients (which may improve competitive position). The system objectives should enable the business objectives: thus the salespeople may be given lap-top computers so that they can produce proposals faster (a system objective), so that the average cost per proposal can be reduced (a business objective) and the win rate can be increased, so that revenue will be increased (a business objective).

The MIS team can responsibly commit to achieving system objectives, but only the business people, led by the Steering Body, can turn those system objectives into the achievement of business objectives. If the salesman chooses not to use the lap-top, the MIS people cannot be held responsible for failure to achieve the business objectives. (They could be held responsible for not delivering a system that was feasible to use.)

The members of the Steering Body do not have the time to specify details of the system requirements such as the exact rules for calculating discounts, or the details of screen layouts. For this, the most knowledgeable clerical or supervisory people - usually termed User Representatives - need to be made available to the project team. As is always the case, the best people to play this role are often the busiest and most critical to their business units, precisely because of their business knowledge. Waiting for them to give spare time to help in specifying requirements delays the project; people who "can be spared" often do not know how the business should really work, or what data is really needed.

Just as the Executive Sponsor should pick the right managers to be on the Steering Body, so each Steering Body member should pick the best people in each unit to be User Representatives, and should see that their time is made available to the project.

Reference

2-1   Cleland, D.I. and King, W.R. (Eds.) *Project Management Handbook*. New York: Van Nostrand 1983

Exercises and discussion topics

1.   Review some information systems projects with which you are familiar.

   1.1   On each project, what were the resistances to change, and the pressures for change?   How did they affect the progress and success of the project?   Could they have been identified at the start of the project?

   1.2   In the light of this chapter, did any of the projects have a correct management structure?   For those projects which did not have a correctly-chosen Executive Sponsor, how did this affect the progress of the project?

   1.3   For each project, with hindsight, who should have been the Executive Sponsor?   Who should have been on the Steering Body?

2.   Consider a project which you are just starting or may be involved with in the future.

   2.1   Produce a version of the memo to the selected Executive Sponsor, (page 2-7), customized for the project.

   2.2   Plan a presentation to the person who should be Executive Sponsor, selling him/her on the need for such involvement.

   2.3   If your chosen Executive Sponsor declines, who is the next best person?   What do you believe will be the difference in the progress and success of the project if the second-choice person plays the role, as opposed to the first-choice?

Chapter 3

Accelerated analysis: impartial-leader group interviews

3.1   Background

As we noted in Chapter 1, the technique of discovering requirements through a group session arose from dissatisfaction with the conventional serial interviewing process, where one or more analysts interview the Steering Body and the User Representatives one at a time. Apart from the long calendar time required by serial interviewing, it can be hard to resolve differences of viewpoints among different users, especially where several analysts are doing the interviewing. User A can't hear what User B is saying; if their needs are properly reflected in the requirements document, they may be able to pick up differences when they review it, but all too often disagreements about the system do not surface until it is being installed.

(Serial interviewing, however, is not all bad. It does tend to minimize user time commitment: in general, group workshops save calendar time at the price of greater expenditure of user man-hours.)

In the late 1970s, the group dynamics approach, stemming from the work of Warren Bennis (Ref 3-1) and others, was applied to this area. The essence of the group dynamics approach may be expressed in 4 principles:

1.   The conventional meeting with the most senior person taking the chair is not the most productive approach to problem solving. A meeting is most productive when led by a facilitator, who is

> "a neutral servant of the group and does not evaluate or contribute ideas. The responsibility of the facilitator is to help the group focus its energies on a task by suggesting methods and procedures, protecting all members of the group from attack, and making sure that everyone has an opportunity to participate." (Ref 3-2)

2.   The most productive group decision is a consensus in which everyone feels that they have won, or at least feels that even if they have not got exactly what they wanted,   they can accept the decision without compromising any strong convictions or needs.   The session leader may say to each group member, "I know this isn't exactly what you want, but can you live with it?"   If such a "win/win" solution can be devised, it is better than a "win/lose" result,   (which might come from putting the decision to a vote or having the chairperson decide),   because the people who perceive they have lost out will not be motivated to make the solution work.

3.   A group session is most productive if it keeps to an agenda which itself has been arrived at by group consensus.

4.   A group session is most productive if the results of discussions are displayed on the wall as they emerge, where everyone can see them, rather than being in minutes of the meeting circulated later.   The display is sometimes referred to as the "group memory," and the member of the group who creates it plays the role of "scribe" or "recorder."

The initial work of applying these insights to information systems development was done by a group led by Chuck Morris of IBM; the analysis methodology which they developed came to be called Joint Application Design (JAD).

The results were so encouraging that a project was formed within the IBM user organization GUIDE, to pool experiences; this working group has produced several papers (most recently Ref 3-3).   Several consulting firms have been formed by people with experience in using JAD in firms such as IBM, CNA, and AT&T, to provide facilitators on a consulting basis, or to train people to be session leaders.   (Three of these firms are listed at the end of this chapter.)

3.2   Types of workshop session

A typical information systems project involves several group sessions or workshops.   Clearly, the agenda for a workshop session will vary depending on the participants and the nature of the project.   Three broad types of sessions can be distinguished:

1.   Strategy sessions, which discuss project scope, objectives, resources, policy issues, and organizational change issues.   The first such session should be kicked-off by the Executive Sponsor, who may choose to stay for the whole session.   Normally, participants include all the Steering Body, any other relevant user managers and experts, plus the MIS Project Manager and analysts.   Depending on the significance of the system, the Manager of Systems Development and the Data Administrator may also take part.   Strategy sessions may use data flow diagrams and entity-relationship diagrams to express project scope.

2.   Data/process sessions, which build or refine data flow diagrams and data models, and define business policy logic, such as the rules for accruing depreciation or the rules for allowing credit.   Participants may include interested heads of departments (who may be Steering Body members) and supervisory/clerical User Representatives.

3.   Screens-and-reports sessions, which (often using prototyping tools), define the interactive dialogues and report layouts that make up the inputs and outputs on the system DFD.   Participants are normally clerical User Representatives, including representative people drawn from the group(s) who will have to use the dialogues and reports in their work.

A project may only require one strategy session, with multiple data/process sessions and multiple screens-and-reports sessions.

A workshop session may produce actual (draft) deliverables, such as data flow diagrams, lists of data elements, approved prototype dialogues, and so on. While desirable, such deliverables are not mandatory: the basic output of a group session consists of the raw material for a deliverable (just as the basic output of an interview is the raw material of an analyst's notes).

The workshop session should be thought of as basically replacing the requirements-gathering functions of the conventional serial interview: in many cases it can achieve much more, in terms of creative business problem solving and conflict resolution, but the minimum to be expected is the output of conventional interviews, delivered in less calendar time.

3.3 The role of the session leader (facilitator)

As can be gauged from the four principles of group dynamics, the success of a workshop session is critically dependent on the interactive skills and preparation of the facilitator. The session leader (SL) has important work to do before and after the workshop session.

Before the workshop:

1.   The SL should learn as much about the business area and the project as the available materials will allow.

2.   The SL (accompanied by the MIS Project Manager) should interview each designated participant briefly.

     For a strategy session, the SL should get the participant's view of the problems that the proposed system should solve, the benefits a system should provide, and identify any potential areas of conflict. If possible, these issues should be resolved by the Executive Sponsor before the session.

     Before all sessions, the SL should understand each participant's function and ideas about the proposed system. Where a person has not been in a workshop on the project before, the SL should brief them on the current status of the project, and on the nature and purpose of the session. If the person has never been in an impartial-leader group session before, the SL should explain the ground-rules to them.

3.   The SL should work out a detailed draft agenda for the workshop.

During the workshop:

1.   The SL should review the status of the project.

2.   On the first strategy session, the Executive Sponsor should state the goals of the project, and lay down any relevant policy issues. He should remind everyone that he is taking a personal interest in and responsibility for the success of the project, and will be continually available to resolve any issues that the group cannot deal with. As noted above, the Executive Sponsor may leave at this point, or may choose to remain in the strategy session.

3. The MIS Project Manager may comment on technological issues, for example, if new developments now make a system feasible that was not previously affordable. The new development(s) (for example, portable computers, voice recognition, expert systems and so on) may be demonstrated to the group.

4. The SL should review the ground rules for the session, and allow the group to modify them, if they want to.

5. The SL should review the draft agenda, and facilitate the reaching of a consensus on the agenda.

6. The SL should facilitate discussion of each point on the agenda, allowing reasonable flexibility, but seeking always to keep the discussion moving forward, and to the point. He should encourage quiet members of the group to get involved ("Do you agree with what has been said so far?"), help verbose members to be succinct ("I hear you saying X. Is that correct?"), and mediate conflicts to reach a win/win consensus ("Can everyone live with that?"). Where agreement cannot be reached, the SL should record the issue, to be resolved after the workshop.

7. The SL is also responsible for directing the scribe(s), who may write on flipcharts or magnetic displays, or use automated graphics/text software on a PC to build projected images.

After the session:

1. The SL should help the MIS Project Manager and the project team to digest the material which has been produced.

2. The SL should do whatever is necessary (for example, meet with Executive Sponsor and selected members of the Steering Body) to make sure that issues that came up but were not resolved during the session are handled quickly and effectively.

3.4 Facilitating vs. chairing a meeting

The most distinctive feature of this technique is the use of an impartial facilitator (which is why this book refers to the approach as that of "impartial-leader group interviews").

The technique is different from that of a "well-run chaired-meeting" (using some version of Robert's Rules of Order).

In a "chaired meeting"

1. Someone, usually the most senior person in the room, takes the chair, and presents the agenda. The chairperson calls on people to speak, and can cut off discussion either by making a decision, or by putting the issue to a vote. The chairperson may generate a "phony consensus" by saying "I think what we should do is X. Are we all agreed?" which puts anyone who does not agree in the position of having to publicly oppose their superior. Participants are always wondering to themselves, "Should I tell him what I really think, or should I tell him what he wants to hear?"

2. The chairperson usually has a strong interest in the content of the result, and so will naturally tend to bias the discussion in that direction. Good ideas and important, though unwelcome, facts may be suppressed.

3. Where the chairperson is the decision maker, he is combining the work of controlling the discussion with the more critical job of assimilating suggestions and views to come up with the best decision. A decision-making chairperson may suffer overload, and so not arrive at the best outcome.

In a "facilitated meeting"

1. The work of controlling the discussion is done by someone whose interest is in making sure all views are heard, rather than in the specific outcome. The facilitator concentrates on the process of the session, rather than on the content. (In some cases, a facilitator can be helpful without even understanding much about the subject matter!)

2. The facilitator should have (or quickly gain) everyone's respect, but has no formal authority over the participants. It's easier for a person to speak freely when called on by an impartial facilitator, than when called on by their boss, even if their boss is in the group.

3. The facilitator can try to devise "win-win" solutions to conflicts that everyone can live with, rather than making command decisions, or putting matters to a vote, as in a chaired meeting.

For a full discussion of these issues, see Reference 3-2.

3.5   Where do session leaders come from?

Clearly, the quality of the SL is critical in having a successful impartial-leader group interview.   If the SL fails to gain trust and respect, or fails to resolve conflicts, or allows discussions to wander, a lot of expensive people-time is wasted and the project suffers a serious setback.   (This is the major risk in using the technique.)

An SL should be highly verbal, quick-thinking on his feet, able to listen and grasp quickly what people mean and are feeling: a DP background is helpful, but not essential for someone with very strong interpersonal skills.

SLs are typically either consultants (from specialized consulting firms or internal groups), or are MIS Project Managers from other projects, playing the role on a part-time basis.   Being an SL is very draining: most people cannot do it for long on anything near a full-time basis without becoming burnt-out.   Reports indicate that it may become a transitional assignment: people spend 12-18 months as a session leader, during which time they impress a number of senior executives with their ability.

References

3-1   Schein, E. and Bennis, W.   *Personal and Organizational Change Through Group Methods*. New York: Wiley, 1965

3-2   Doyle, M. and Straus, D.   *How to Make Meetings Work*.   New York: Berkley/Jove, 1976

3-3   GUIDE Publication GPP-147.   *Joint Application Design*.   Chicago: GUIDE International, 1986

Some consulting firms specializing in accelerated analysis:

JA Tech Designer Systems
461 Lakeshore Road W
Oakville, ON   L6K 1G4, Canada
416/845-3844

MG Rush Systems
2201 Chestnut Drive
Bloomfield Hills, MI 48013
313/433-FAST

Performance Resources Inc.
5111 Leesburg Pike
Falls Church, VA 22041
703/845-9600

Exercise and discussion topics:

1.   Review some projects you are familiar with which used serial interviewing. Were there any issues or conflicts between different users that serial interviewing did not identify, but which you believe would have been resolved in a group interview?

2.   With a group of associates, read and discuss the paperback by Doyle and Straus, "How to make meetings work," (available from Berkley/Jove, 200 Madison Avenue, New York, NY 10016 for $4.50). Take turns to be the facilitator for a discussion in the group. Have the group give each facilitator feedback on their effectiveness.

3.   Review GUIDE publication GPP-147, and make contact with people in other organizations who are using JAD or some other impartial-leader group interview technique.

Chapter 4

Logical modelling: data flow diagrams

The data flow diagram (DFD) is the primary planning tool for an information system. The DFD shows the boundary of the system: whatever is not an external entity is inside. The DFD is uniquely important because it is the only document that shows all the relationships between the data (data stores and data flows) and the processes and functions that transform that data.

4.1   Conventions

Since the DFD's symbols are non-physical, it shows the underlying logical essence of the information system, and therefore is highly meaningful to business people whether or not they know anything about computers. After a minute or two's explanation of the symbols, anyone who can read a map can read a dataflow.

4.1.1 External entities (EEs)

The conventional symbol is a square given solidity by shading on two sides. Often the external entity is given an identifying letter, M for Management, C for Customers, and so on.

External entities are sources and/or destinations of flows of data into and out of the system. They are, by definition, outside the system under consideration. It's helpful to consider the external entity as being "behind a hole in a wall." That is to say, the system knows nothing about what is going on in the external entity.   Data comes into the system through the hole in the wall;   what happened to it before it came into the system does not concern us.   Data from the system goes back through the hole in the wall and disappears;   we are not concerned with what becomes of it.   Data comes into the system only from external entities - it goes out of the system only to external entities.

If, as an analyst, you find yourself describing what goes on inside an external entity, you need to recognize that your system boundary really is wider than you are presently considering.

The external entity may be physically represented by a group of people, such as customers, or perhaps a system, such as a payroll system.   It may be just one person: the President or Comptroller.   It sometimes happens that the same group/person/system that is an external entity is also involved in implementing a process in the system.   For example, if management receives sales analysis reports, as shown here:

they may also be the agent that sets the safety levels for inventory reordering, as indicated by the lower portion of the process block, shown here:

It sometimes happens that a data flow will go out to an external entity, and then come back into the system again, but in an altered form, possibly with a completely different name.   In the example below, expense items are going out to the Accounts Department which is "behind the wall" as an External Entity, and a data flow is reappearing which on examination turns out to be the same expense items with general ledger codes added to them.

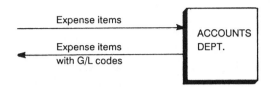

One has to ask, "Does this external entity conceal a process which could usefully be part of the system?" Additionally one might ask, "In testing the system, does the analyst have to test that the coding of expense items is done correctly?" The coding process might well be a candidate for automation, in which case it should be brought into the system and analyzed as part of it.

Sometimes, for clarity, it's necessary to duplicate external entities to prevent long data flow arrows going from one side of a diagram to another. This is conventionally done by putting a diagonal stroke in the bottom right-hand corner of the external entity symbol, which says to the reader of the diagram, "there is more than one of this entity."

On very large diagrams it may be convenient to put a number inside the triangle to show how many instances of the entity there are. Of course, if this is done, and then another instance of the symbol is added, all the numbers in all the instances of the symbol will need to be updated.

4.1.2 Data flows

Unlike an arrow on a conventional flowchart, which shows the transfer of control from one program step or module to another, the arrow on a DFD is to be thought of as a pathway, down which one or more data structures may pass as some unspecified time. As we shall see later, the timing of the flow of data and the operation of the processes is dealt with in the specification of the processes themselves. A data flow diagram resembles a railroad map; it shows where the train tracks are laid, but it does not give the time tables.

Usually each data flow arrow has a name which describes only one data structure. Sometimes, several similar data structures may be shown passing down the same data flow, as shown here:

It's often convenient to have two-headed arrows on a diagram used as a shorthand for two separate arrows, as the example shows:

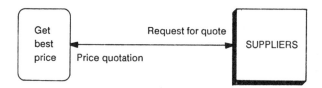

Maintaining a top-to-bottom, left-to-right convention, the "Request for Quotation" is to be read as going along the implied left-to-right arrow. It is helpful to put the name of each data flow nearer the relevant arrow-head, as shown.

If, at some later stage, you come to formally document the data flows, you must recognize that, really, two separate arrows exist here.

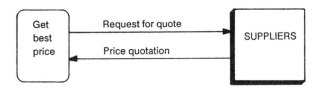

Branching arrows mean that the same data flow is going from one origin to two different places, as shown in this example:

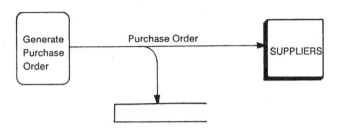

Purchase orders are being sent to suppliers, and the same data stored in a data store.

As a general rule, a DFD has more clarity if the data flows go only horizontally and vertically, with curved corners; however, diagonal arrows may be drawn when it is clearer to do so.

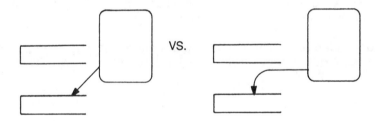

Where data flows cross without meeting, either a hoop (jumping over) or a gap (tunnelling under) may be used.

Where the contents of a dataflow will be obvious to everyone who will look at the diagram, it need not necessarily be named. Particularly in a relational environment, this book takes the view that it is often not worth the effort of documenting the contents of data flow arrows, provided the contents of the associated table(s) are defined.

Nonetheless, it is essential for the analyst to be able to answer the question "What do you mean by this?" for any given data flow arrow on any data flow diagram. If the analyst who drew the diagram cannot define what passes down a dataflow, one has to ask "Why not?" Often it's because the arrow has been drawn, not to signify data flow, but to signify control transfer or sequence, as shown in the example here:

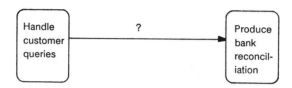

No information flows from the process, "Handle customer queries," to the process, "Produce bank reconciliation." The arrow, however, was drawn to represent the fact that in this organization, the bank reconciliation is not produced until the end of the day when the person who has been handling customer queries is free to do the work. The arrow, therefore, is a completion signal which represents a timing consideration due to the particular physical implementation of the system. It is not a flow of data.

If timing dependencies are important to the analysis, as they often are, a timing chart should be developed, as shown in the diagram:

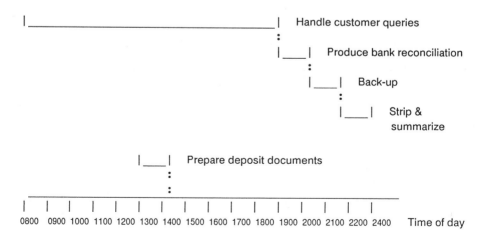

4.1.3 Processes

A process or function which transforms data in some way is normally represented by a rectangle with rounded corners, as shown in the diagram. (A rectangle is easier to write in than a circle, which some writers use.)

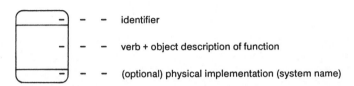

- - - identifier

- - - verb + object description of function

- - - (optional) physical implementation (system name)

The upper portion of the symbol normally carries an identifying number.

The body of the symbol should have a description of the function of the process, starting with a verb, followed by an object clause, such as "Generate" (the verb), "sales transactions," (the object clause).

The lower portion may, optionally, contain the department or the program or some other agent which physically implements the process in the system.

On a system-wide DFD, we are aiming to show all the function and data of a given information system on a single "small-scale map." The clustering of function into named processes should be such that if the business logic of a process were to be written out in full, it would take up not less than one page, normally not more than 5 pages, very exceptionally up to 10 pages.

A process such as "Extend item total" which written out in full becomes just one line ("Multiply unit price by quantity ordered") is much too trivial for a system-wide DFD. On the other hand, a process such as "Plan production" could easily require 20-30 pages to describe. Such a process should either be divided into several smaller process blocks, or should be "exploded" into a more detailed data flow diagram showing the inner details of the process block itself, as described in the next Section.

Processes should not be duplicated, unless identical processes, such as "Update accounts receivable" are used in widely different parts of the system, and the long data flow arrows that result are too confusing (even using on-page connectors). Where duplication cannot be avoided, the same convention may be used as with external entities: a diagonal line in the bottom right-hand corner.

As a general rule, error and exception flows should not be shown on a system-wide DFD unless they are very significant to the user community. The system-wide DFD is intended as a working planning tool, not a comprehensive specification: the aim is to show the normal flow of normal data. Error and exception handling should be deferred until the details of procedure units are specified.

It is often useful to have a one- or two-paragraph description of each process, which can easily be referred to while reading a DFD. This "process summary" may be stored in a data dictionary (if one is used), or in a word processor file. (Of course, if process definitions and narratives are put in a data dictionary, it becomes more than just a *data* dictionary, but the term has come to be used for "a place to store information about data and processes.") This process summary is not to be confused with the full detail of process logic, as discussed in Chapter 10.

4.1.4 Data stores

A data store, the symbol for which is an elongated rectangle, is chosen to represent one or more tables in a relational database.

In principle, every table can be represented as a separate data store on a DFD. However, where two or more tables represent data about the same entity (often a master/detail structure such as SALES and SALES_ITEMS) and so are usually accessed together, it is more compact to put them in the same data store. Such a data store is named by the names of the tables with a ' / ' separator, as shown here:

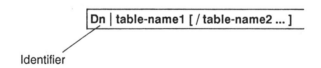

If the concatenated names of the tables are too long for the symbol, the most general table name may be used, with a + sign, and the other tables listed underneath thus:

> | table-name1 +
>
> table-name2
> table-name3

Data stores may be duplicated to avoid tangled data flows. The symbol for duplication is a triangle added to the left hand end of the data store symbol. As with external entities, on a large diagram the number of instances of the data store may be given in the triangle:

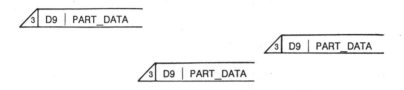

Data stores can be thought of as holding information about either objects (such as PRODUCTS or SUPPLIERS), which endure over time, or events (such as SALES or PURCHASES), which occur at a point in time.

Where the data store is storing data about an object it will typically be subject to a fairly low volume of routine maintenance transactions. In the case of customers, there would be new customers, changes of customer address, and deletions of inactive customers. Normally, these routine maintenance flows are shown by at least one external entity feeding data into a process which updates the data store, thus:

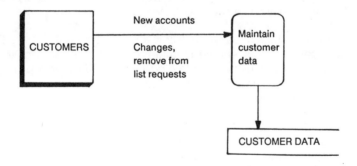

As a shorthand notation, these routine maintenance data flows and processes may be omitted from the DFD and shown by the letters, RM, attached to the data store symbol, as shown:

RM
CUSTOMER DATA

This implies that there is at least one process which is not shown on the DFD, but which must be physically implemented in the eventual system.

Data stores that are shared with other systems

Particularly in a relational database environment where a number of systems may share the same database, the system being defined may read and update data stores which are also read and/or updated by other related systems. It's convenient to be able to show this explicitly on a DFD.

Two situations can be distinguished:

1. Where a data store is maintained by another system and our system only reads it, the convention is as shown:

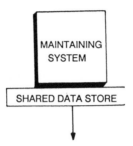

Logically speaking, the data store belongs to the maintaining system. Our system has no responsibility for it.

The data from it comes as though from "behind the wall." In this case, however, the data store is shown to make evident the name of the table(s) which are to be read. In the maintain*ing* system DFD, the process which updates that data store should be shown and our system should appear as an external entity, having read-only access to it:

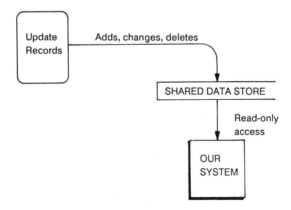

2.   If both the systems update the data store,   then the notation shown
        below should be used:

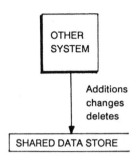

Additions, changes and deletions (as appropriate) should be shown coming
from the other system to the shared data store.

This notation is an exception to the rule that data should not go directly from an
external entity to a data store,   without going through a process which is
responsible for the data transfer.

Search arguments

When data is retrieved from a data store, it is usually on the basis of some
condition.

> SELECT * FROM CUSTOMERS WHERE CUST_ID = 'A94706'

in a SQL statement which will retrieve all the data for the specified customer.
The value of CUST_ID, A94706, is the *search argument*.

> SELECT * FROM PRODUCTS WHERE PRICE > 100
>   AND MARGIN_PERCENT > 10

will retrieve all the corresponding product data.   Here the columns PRICE and
MARGIN_PERCENT provide the search arguments for the table PRODUCTS.

As we shall see in Chapter 8, it is important to know all the search arguments
which are used on each table in a relational database since each such column
is a candidate for the creation of an index.

Search arguments may be shown on a DFD like this:

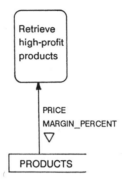

Single-inflow, single-outflow data stores

Any data store with only one flow going into it, and only one flow coming out of it, should be examined to see whether the storage of data is logically necessary for a business reason, or whether the data store only exists to represent a temporary physical file which exists just because of the way the system is/will be implemented.

For example, a floppy disk which is created to carry data from branch office to head office does not represent a storage of data which is logically necessary for the business: the data could be transferred over a telephone line. The floppy disk in this case is just a temporary physical file being used for data transfer. On the other hand, a floppy disk holding details of customers with poor credit ratings, which are held until the Credit Manager has an opportunity to review them, *would* be logically necessary to reflect the way the business is conducted, even though it only has one inflow and one outflow.

4.2 Fission, explosion and levelling

As was mentioned in the discussion of the process symbol in the previous section, it is good practice to keep processes to a manageable size, even on a system-wide DFD. A "manageable size" corresponds to between 1 and 5 (exceptionally up to 10) pages of business logic.

If a process is discovered which the analyst thinks exceeds a manageable size, there are two alternatives: fission and explosion.

With fission, the original process of, say, 20 pages of logic is replaced on the system-wide DFD by, say, 5 processes, each of 4 pages of logic.

With explosion, the original process remains on the system-wide DFD but a new lower-level DFD is created, consisting of less complex processes, and any data stores which turn out to be necessary, but were not discovered in the development of the system-wide DFD.

The diagram on the next page shows an explosion of Process 5, "Analyze shipments" from the DFD used in Chapter 1. As in the system-wide diagram, shipment information is received from suppliers, and used in sub-process 5.1 and sub-process 5.2.

Sub-process 5.1 uses SUPPLIER_ID as a search argument to retrieve all outstanding purchase orders for that supplier and also to retrieve all past deliveries for those purchase orders; it thus identifies the purchase orders which have not been fully delivered.

Sub-process 5.2 (presumably manual) checks the shipment for breakages, and counts the number of each product delivered. If there are any breakages, a report to the supplier is created in sub-process 5.5.

Sub-process 5.3 applies the unbroken quantity of each product to the unfilled purchase order(s). If the amount shipped is correct, or still not enough to completely satisfy what is on order, a delivery record is created and inserted into the deliveries table. If the quantity received is *greater* than that which is on order, the details of relevant purchase orders and deliveries are put in D7: OVERSHIPMENTS, where they are stored until the Buying Manager has an opportunity to review them, and to decide (in sub-process 5.6, given current inventories and recent sales) whether to accept any overshipments or return them.

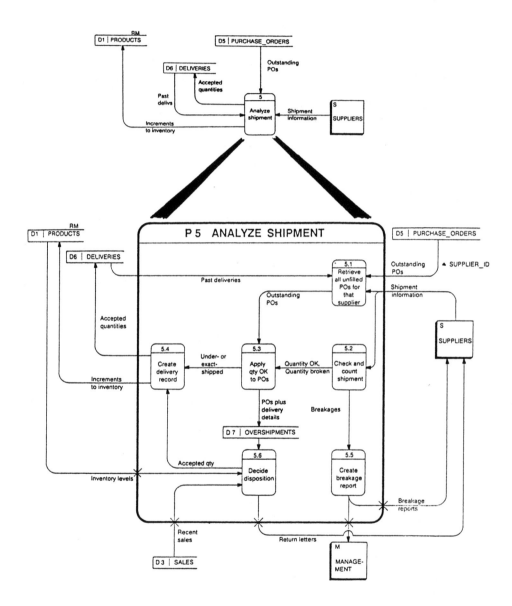

Note that the explosion diagram deals with the possible exception conditions, such as products being received broken, or more products being received than were ordered. It includes a data store D7, (required for exception handling), which was not identified on the system-wide diagram. Note also that while all the 3 inflows to, and 2 outflows from, process 5 are also shown on the explosion DFD, there are 2 additional inflows and 3 additional outflows dealing with exception handling (marked with an X where they cross the explosion boundary). Some analysts take the view that, once discovered, all these flows should also be shown on the system-wide diagram, so that the inflows to and outflows from the high-level process exactly balance those crossing the explosion boundary. This book takes the position that the system-wide DFD is primarily a planning tool, and so should show only the normal flow of normal data.

It follows that every inflow and outflow on a high-level process should appear on an explosion diagram, but not vice versa. If explosion is unavoidable, the multi-level set of diagrams will therefore balance downwards, but not upwards.

Several writers on structured analysis (such as Reference 4-1) have recommended extensive use of explosion, suggesting that no DFD should have more than 7 or so processes. This means that any significant system has to be represented by a multi-level package of DFDs. A system with 50 processes would, in principle, be represented by 8 DFDs: one DFD to show the most general view of the system, and 7 more to show the explosions of the high-level processes.

This book takes the opposite position, that explosion should be avoided if at all possible. An information system should be represented by a single system-wide data flow diagram of whatever size necessary, with each process representing between 1 and 5 pages of business logic. A diagram only 17" by 22" can hold 100 process symbols and their corresponding data stores without undue crowding. If each such process corresponds to 5 pages of logic then this single system-wide DFD summarizes 500 pages of logic. Only the very largest and most complex systems need to resort to explosion.

The not-so-magical number 7, plus or minus 2

If you say to someone, "43279: what did I just say?", almost everyone can repeat the number back correctly. On the other hand, if you say "292245887", the 9 meaningless digits exceed many people's short-term memory.

Experiments like these (Ref 4-2) show that people (and many animals) have several perception processes which can handle between 5 and 9 (7 +/- 2) things at once.

This finding has been used as a justification for modelling systems with multiple simple DFDs. However, one is not required to hold the whole of a DFD in short-term memory. One may attend to an area of a DFD, or an area of a map, which holds only 9 symbols, and then switch attention to another area. But this very switching of attention means that a static 2-dimensional display can be quite complex, especially if one of its important aspects is the way in which all the parts are connected.

To select the best Interstate highway route from Miami to Seattle, one needs a nation-wide map, showing the 48 states and over 200 cities. It would be very difficult to plan a route if the country were broken down into 7 regional maps, with each region broken down into areas, each containing only 7 cities. Such fragmentation destroys the topology, or connectedness, of the display.

The objection is sometimes made that a system-wide DFD will not fit into a binder holding 8 1/2" by 11" documentation. True, but what is the practice in construction and engineering? Blueprints are referred to in documents, and stored folded or rolled. The system-wide DFD is the blueprint for its information system, and should be handled in a similar way.

4.3   Review criteria for DFDs

Once you have drafted a DFD, or when you are reviewing DFDs drafted by others, it's useful to have a checklist to prompt you to look for some of the more obvious errors that can be made:

- Do all processes have a description with the structure "Verb + Noun-clause object?"

- Do all data stores represent objects or events of interest?
  If not, can the developer explain their contents?

- Do all processes and data stores have at least one inflow and one outflow? If not, why not?

- Can the developer explain all unnamed data flows?

- Do all data flows start or end with a process?
  If not, what makes them happen?

- Do all data flows have at least one arrowhead?

■   Are there any data stores with only one inflow and one outflow which are temporary physical intermediate files?

Suppose we apply this checklist to the DFD below.

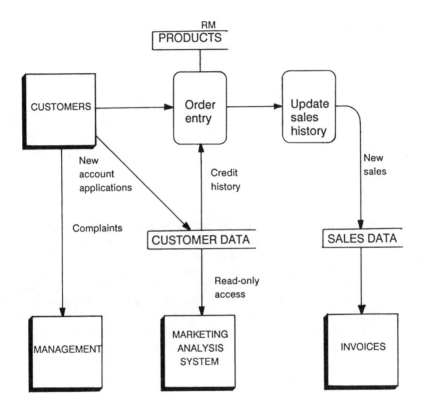

We will see that:

1.   Complaints are shown going directly from CUSTOMERS to MANAGEMENT i.e. from one external entity to another.   If this is true, then complaints are not part of the system under consideration and so should not be shown.   If they *are* part of the system, then they should be shown as being handled by some process in the system.

2.   The data flow from data store PRODUCTS has no arrowhead or description.

3.   The data flow from SALES_DATA to the external entity INVOICES has no description.   This would be acceptable provided the analyst could explain what went down it.   But INVOICES is not an allowable name for an external entity;   It's neither a group of people nor a system.   We suspect that the data flow is actually "Invoices" and that the external entity should be CUSTOMERS.

4.   New account applications are shown going directly from the external entity CUSTOMERS to CUSTOMER_DATA, without being processed in any way.   If the external entity CUSTOMERS were a system maintaining CUSTOMER_DATA, this would be acceptable, but of course it's not.

5.   The process "Order entry" is not named with a verb-plus-object description.   It should be renamed "Enter orders."   Though the distinction is trivial in this case, "Order Entry" may be the name of a department, which implies a physical implementation, rather than a logical process.

Of course, these are only syntactical points: the DFD may also be wrong because it doesn't reflect what the business does, or covers the wrong part of the business, or doesn't make sense to people who know the application.   The processes may be poorly chosen. For example, "Enter orders" might have 15 pages of logic associated with it, while "Update sales history" might only need 3 lines.   A DFD must be semantically correct - must tell the truth in a way meaningful to its audience - as well as being syntactically correct.   But as with a written statement in English, one first attends to the syntax, and then considers whether what is being said is meaningful and correct.

4.4   Techniques for developing DFDs

Layout

DFDs are more readable if the external entities are arranged around the outside of the diagram, so that the implicit system boundary lies immediately inside the ring of external entities.   While it's not absolutely necessary, it is helpful if the main transaction flow goes from the left hand side of the diagram towards the right.   Readers thus get used to looking at the left side of the diagram, to find the external entity which is the source of the transactions that drive the system.

Many transaction processing systems can be seen as resembling this very general schematic:

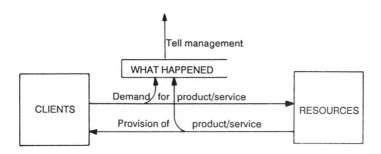

Some group of clients demands a product or service.   The information system has to process these demands (for example, sales orders from customers), and translate them into a form where a demand can be placed on the resource(s) (employees, suppliers) which are the ultimate source of the products or services.   The external entities corresponding to these resources are at the right side of the diagram.   As the resources provide the products or services, and they are delivered to the clients, there is another flow of information through the system.   Both flows of information cause data about what happened to be stored, and information about demand, provision, clients and resources to be spun off to management (typically located at the top and bottom of the diagram).

Of course, not all systems are like this.   Decision support systems typically use data which has already been stored as a result of some earlier transaction flow. Process control systems are quite different.   But the general "Clients-demands-resources-provision" model is common enough to be useful, and using the standard layout can help comprehension.

Duplications of symbols should be kept to a minimum, consistent with having an acceptable number of data flow lines crossing one another.

The External Entity/Input/Output (EEIO) listing.

Except where a DFD is very simple, it is a good idea to start out by producing an EEIO listing. This simply identifies what you believe are the external entities of the system, and lists the inputs that you know come from them, together with the outputs that you know will go to them.

Taking the DFD used in Chapter 1, the EEIO listing would look like:

External Entity	Input from	Output to
CUSTOMERS	Sales orders	
BANK		Deposit documents
MANAGEMENT		Sales data
SUPPLIERS	Shipment information	Purchase orders

(In practice, of course, the list would be much longer.)

First draft DFD

Since the development of a data flow diagram is essentially an act of discovery, the first draft can never be of presentation quality. The purpose of the first draft is to identify all the processes and data stores, and put down the connections between them, however messy the result may be. Later drafts of the DFD can look more polished, depending on the tools available.

The first draft is started by examining the EEIO list to see which input(s) "drive" the system. In the case of the list above, the driving input is clearly "Sales orders."

The external entity that generates this input should be placed in the middle of the left edge of the paper. Then the questions should be asked "What is the logical process that deals with this input?"   "What data stores does this process need in order to function?" "What outputs will the process generate?" The same questions are repeated for each output from the first logical process, and so the first draft is built up.

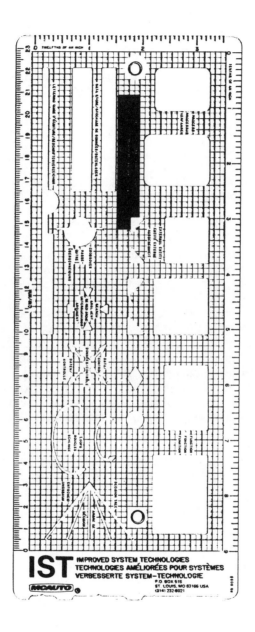

A widely-used template available from the McDonnell Douglas IST Group.

The first draft can be done either as a free-hand sketch, or by using adhesive labels for the symbols, and drawing the data flow lines in very lightly with pencil. Removeable adhesive labels, such as Post-It notes, simplify the task of moving symbols around as better layouts are visualized. The analyst should concentrate on being comprehensive; even if the diagram is a mess, let it be a complete mess. The DFD can then be redrawn for discussion and presentation purposes. For some examples of the development of a DFD, see Reference 4-3.

Later drafts: automated tools

The second, and later drafts, can be produced using a template for the drawing of the symbols, such as the one shown on the previous page.

Alternatively, once a first draft has been produced, an automated graphics tool can be used to enter the diagram into a PC or workstation. Obviously it is easier to make minor changes in a diagram once it is held in machine-readable form. Since diagrams can easily go through 10 to 20 versions in the course of a project, it is clearly more productive to have automated help.

While a general-purpose graphics package (such as AUTOSKETCH) can be used, there are a number of graphics packages which are specifically designed for logical modelling. Most are also integrated with a data dictionary facility which can store the details of the logical model. Some have screen-painting facilities which can be used for prototyping. Beyond this, some products provide interfaces to code-generation packages, or have built-in code generation facilities. Such software packages have come to be known as CASE (Computer-Aided Software Engineering) tools.

More advanced CASE products help the analyst with the syntax of the diagram, warning when, for example, the analyst tries to set up an improper connection, of when an object is left unconnected to the rest of the diagram.

Appendix A discusses the nature of these CASE tools, and suggests criteria for evaluating them.

4.5   Should the current system be modelled?

Throughout our discussion of logical modelling so far, we have been thinking in terms of the system which is to be developed; the proposed or required system.   Often, this proposed system will be replacing an existing, or current system, which may be automated or manual or part-automated, part-manual.

At the logical level, the proposed system often is very similar to the current system.   Often the business has not changed; the same transactions have to be processed, and the same outputs produced.   The new system is being developed to do the same things as the current system, only better and faster, and to capture more data about what is happening.

Consequently, one way of deriving a model of the proposed system is to study the current system, derive a logical model of it, and then ask, "What changes need to be made to the current system logical model, in order that it can meet the objectives of the required system?"   The DFD's may be identical; perhaps it's just that more data will be held about customers, or about suppliers, so that only the current data model will need to be enhanced to make the proposed data model.

In an integrated database environment, it will often be most important to study the current data model(s) to see how the proposed system will fit with them.

If a table describing CUSTOMERS already exists,   and is in use by 17 application systems, then our proposed system should not create a new table to hold the same data unless:

1.   The database administrator decides that for performance or security reasons our system cannot be granted access to an existing table.

2.   The existing table does not hold some data elements that we need in our system, but the database administrator will not give us permission to modify the existing table.

Of course, it's not *necessary* to model the current system.   It's perfectly possible to say, "Forget what we're doing now; in the light of the needs of the business,   what should the future system do?"   and start modelling the proposed system from scratch.

The issue is, "Which is the quickest, most productive way to arrive at the proposed system logical model?"   This question has to be answered for each project, in the light of the information available.   In general terms, if the objective of the project is to make little change in the business functions or data held, it is often quickest to develop a current system model, because tangible information about the current system is easy to come by. If the new system will have several of the same physical interfaces as the old system, these will need to be investigated and understood. On the other hand, if the problem is that the business has changed, or that a new system is needed to do something rather different from the old system, the time spent in modelling the current system may be wasted.

Also, modelling the current system has acquired a bad reputation in some quarters, because it represents a definite familiar task which some analysts have seized on as an excuse to delay confronting the hard issues about the future needs of the business. Developing the current system model is not an end in itself, just a way of getting to the proposed system model.

A related question is "Should the current *physical* system be documented?" If the project is required to replace a running system which has no proper program documentation, how is the process logic to be derived?

In such a situation, it is almost always best to go directly to the proposed logical model if at all possible, working with the best User Representatives to "re-invent" the business logic. If there truly is no-one who understands the business rules built into the current system, for example, how the system computes interest, then it is necessary to go through the time-consuming process of studying the current physical system. If doing so is unavoidable, there are two approaches. The "cold-turkey" approach studies the outputs, deduces from them what data must be stored, and looks at inputs to see how the outputs are derived from the inputs. The "grease-monkey" approach looks at the physical files, and re-documents the logic of the programs to understand the business logic behind them. Sometimes both approaches must be combined. It is rarely easy, and never rapid.

Reverse engineering

However, several projects are underway to automate the "grease-monkey" approach. Some help may be had from software packages which scan source code listings and restructure the code to make it more readable and maintainable.

For example, "Structured Retrofit," marketed by the Catalyst Group of Peat Marwick, will read one or more COBOL programs, whatever their control flow structure, and produce a revised version of each program, improving the clarity and readability of the code. It replaces all ALTER statements, removes unreachable ("dead") code, restricts the use of GO TO statements, and rewrites the program as a hierarchical modular structure.

More ambitiously, Charles W. Bachman's group (with which the present writer is associated) is developing a family of expert-system-based CASE products, which will analyze programs and database definitions, and extract their underlying process logic and data structures to make a logical model of a current system with the minimum human intervention. After the current system has been reverse engineered in this way, the logical data/process model can be changed, and then a new system forward engineered by automatic creation of database definitions and program code.

References:

4-1   DeMarco, T.   *Structured Analysis and System Specification.* Englewood Cliffs, NJ: Prentice-Hall, 1979

4-2   Miller, G. A.   *The magical number seven, plus or minus two.* Psychological Review, Vol. 63, March 1956

4-3   Gane, C. and Sarson, T.   *Structured Systems Analysis: tools and techniques.* Englewood Cliffs, NJ: Prentice-Hall, 1979

Exercises and discussion topics:

1.   Select a system which you know well, and prepare a system-wide data flow diagram to depict its underlying logical essence, using the guidelines given in this Chapter. How may processes do you find are necessary? How many data stores?

2.   Draw a timing chart for the system you used in 1.

3.   Take a package of "levelled" data flow diagrams, and redraw them to make one system-wide DFD. Ask two sets of people to answer the same questions, in one case using the single-sheet system-wide DFD, in another case using the levelled DFD package. What differences in speed and comprehension do you find?

4.   Compare the time needed to draw a DFD:

   a)   using a template
   b)   using any CASE tool available to you.

   For each version, compare the time taken to produce a new version which involves:

   a)   adding one more process and one more data store
   b)   moving several processes from one side of the diagram to another.

Chapter 5

Logical modelling:
entity-relationship diagrams

5.1   What is an entity? What is a relationship?

As we saw in Chapter 1, entity-relationship (E-R) analysis is a valuable way of getting insights into the overall structure of the data represented by a system or business area.   E-R analysis *can* be done based just on one's knowledge of the business, but this book recommends that it be done after the initial data flow diagram has been drafted.

As we discussed in Chapter 1, the key question is: "What entities are of such an interest to the business, that in order to meet the system's objectives, we need to store data about them?"   Entities are usually objects or events, for example, customers, suppliers, parts, products, people.   Objects endure over time.   Events occur at a specific moment.   An object may have two or more events associated with it (the start and finish of a project;   the hiring and termination of an employee).   An event may represent an association between two or more objects (a customer ordering a product, an employee working on a project).

It's worth keeping in mind the fact that each entity is going to end up being represented by at least one table.   Consequently, something which does not involve at least two data elements to describe it, is probably not an entity, but an attribute of something else or just a data element on its own.   For example while, on the strict definition, HIRE DATE could be considered as an entity, it consists of only one data element, presumably describing an employee, and so would not be a very meaningful entity.   The color "red" is not an entity: it could be a value of an attribute of an entity.

As a rule of thumb, if you cannot imagine the entity you propose as being the name of a data store on a system DFD, it is probably not worth defining as one. Conversely, if each data store does not represent at least one entity, it may not be necessary to the system.   It is also worth reviewing the External Entities on the first-cut DFD, to see whether any of them need to have data stored about them in the system.

Once a list of entities has been drawn up, we look at each pair of entities that we have identified, and ask what relationships, if any, must be recognized between them.

1:1

"Each Division is managed by one, and only one, Manager"
"Each Manager manages one, and only one, Division"

1:Many

"Each Sale involves one or more Sales Items"
"Each Sale Item is part of only one Sale"

Many:Many

"Each Supplier supplies one or more Products"
"Each Product is supplied by one or more Suppliers"

The diagram on the opposite page shows the three types of possible relationships (one-to-one, one-to-many, many-to-many). The presence or absence of an arrowhead, meaning "one" or "many" respectively, is known as the "degree marker," or "cardinality marker." In some notations, as shown in the diagram, the description of the relationship is written along the line which joins the two entities. So the relationship between two entities on this type of diagram can be read in its general form as:

> "Each *entity-name*
> *relationship-description-near-entity*
> *degree-marker-other-end*
> *other-entity*"

Since, in a relational DBMS, the type of relationship ("is managed by," "supplies") is not usually stored, it is not strictly necessary to include it in an E-R diagram, except where there is more than one relationship between two entities. For instance, PRODUCT and SUPPLIER may be associated both by "SUPPLIER offers PRODUCT" and "PRODUCT is actually bought from SUPPLIER" as shown here:

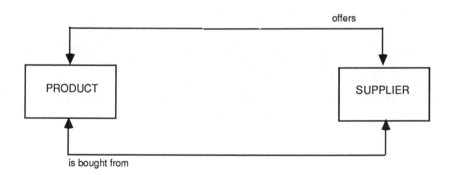

In this case, it is worth including both relationship descriptions; since each relationship will give rise to a different intersection entity (PRODUCT_SOURCE in the case of "offers," PURCHASE_ORDER in the case of "is bought from"). Note that it's only strictly necessary to have a description at one end of the relationship line; you can always infer the description which should go on the other end. (IF SUPPLIERs offer PRODUCTs, then PRODUCTs must be offered by SUPPLIERs, and so on.)

Where there is only one relationship between two entities, a simple line connecting the two is sufficient, and may be read in either direction as "is associated with":

"Each sale is associated with one or more Sales Items"
"Each sales item is associated with only one sale"

Part of the difficulty of defining entities and relationships comes from the fact that what one analyst may see as an entity, another analyst may see as a relationship. This is particularly true of entities which are events, such as sales. Is a sale an entity in its own right, or is it a relationship between a customer and a product? An argument can be made on either side.

For our purposes, we will accept as an entity anything which we believe is going to need one or more tables in the database to hold information about it. For us, therefore, a sale is an entity, not a relationship.

Each type of relationship or association should be analyzed in a different way, as discussed in the next three Sections.

5.2   Analyzing one-to-one relationships

When a one-to-one relationship is detected, the question is, "Are the two entities really distinct or can they be merged?" If they have the same identifying key, as we saw in the case of PRODUCTS and INVENTORY in the example in Chapter 1, there is a strong case for merging the two entities into one.   If, given what you know about the data at this stage, you can envisage holding all the information about products and inventory in one table, then you should merge the two.

Sometimes two entities may be truly distinct, but one entity involves only a few data elements and has no relationship to any other entities in the system.   Take the case of a machine and its fuel mix.

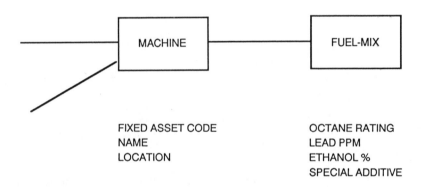

```
FIXED ASSET CODE          OCTANE RATING
NAME                      LEAD PPM
LOCATION                  ETHANOL %
                          SPECIAL ADDITIVE
```

Every machine has its own fuel mix, any one instance of fuel mix relates to one and only one machine, and the fuel mix has no relationship with any other entity in the system.   Consequently, the fuel mix information may well be included as a group of attributes, in with all the other attributes of "machine":

```
FIXED ASSET CODE
NAME
LOCATION
FUEL OCTANE RATING
FUEL LEAD PPM
FUEL ETHANOL %
FUEL SPECIAL ADDITIVE
```

Before making this decision, however, you should ask yourself the key question "Will it always be this way?" If there is any chance that, in the future, one fuel-mix might be used for several machines, or that one machine might have multiple fuel-mixes, then the two entities should be kept separate.

If two entities really *are* distinct, the relationship will have to be maintained in the database by a pointer from one relationship to another. While it's not necessary to document this pointer on the E-R diagram, the analyst should be quite clear what the pointer will be and how the relationship will be maintained.

Take the case of the one-to-one relationship between a division and the person who manages it. Assume that the information, such as name, address and phone for the manager, is stored with that of other employees in a table of PEOPLE, then an identifying pointer, perhaps called the MANAGER_PERSON_ID, would be stored in the table describing the division and would point to the manager's record in the PEOPLE table, as shown in the figure below:

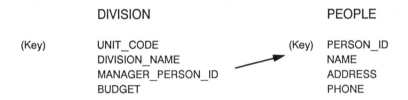

	DIVISION			PEOPLE
(Key)	UNIT_CODE		(Key)	PERSON_ID
	DIVISION_NAME			NAME
	MANAGER_PERSON_ID			ADDRESS
	BUDGET			PHONE

MANAGER_PERSON_ID is referred to as a "foreign key"; that is to say, a data element in DIVISION which is also the key of another table.

An alternative approach would be to include an attribute within the PEOPLE table for the unit which a person manages. That would point to the unit code of the division, in the case of a person who was a manager of that division. For all non-managers, of course, this attribute would be be null.

	DIVISION		PEOPLE
(Key)	UNIT_CODE	(Key)	PERSON_ID
	DIVISION_NAME		NAME
	BUDGET		CODE
			MANAGES_UNIT_CODE

(Note that the foreign keys are named with "qualifier + key-name."   This is a useful convention, which simplifies looking through the data dictionary for all the places where a given key might be referred to.)

While both designs will work, the first one is somewhat more natural. Furthermore, if there is any possibility that one person may ever be the manager of more than one division (perhaps as acting-manager of a second division while a new manager is being recruited), the second design will not allow it, while the first one will.

Once again, this illustrates the point that the analyst should always ask of any one-to-one relationship,   "Will it always be one-to-one?"   "Is there any possibility in the future that it could become one-to-many?"   Choose the design that will best stand up to possible change.

5.3   Analyzing one-to-many relationships

This is the easiest type of relationship to analyze.   Each entity has a table holding its attributes.   The key of the "one" entity is part of the table describing the "many" entity (it may be a part of its key or it may not).

In the example shown below, SALE_NO *is* a part of the key of SALE_ITEMS.

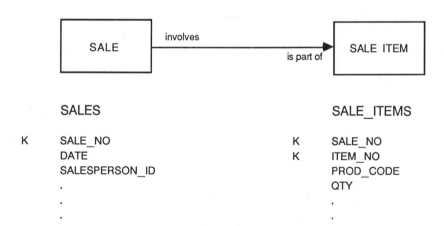

If, on the other hand, we take the example where one customer may have many sales associated with it, CUSTOMER_ID must be part of the sales table, but it is not part of the key, since SALE_NO alone is enough to uniquely identify each sale:

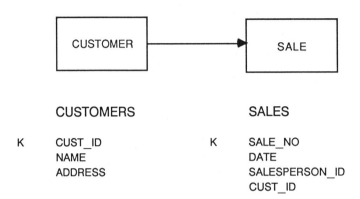

An issue arises when there is a hierarchy of one-to-many relationships.   To continue the example, take the case where one customer may be associated with several sales and each sale may be associated with several items,   as shown in the diagram below:

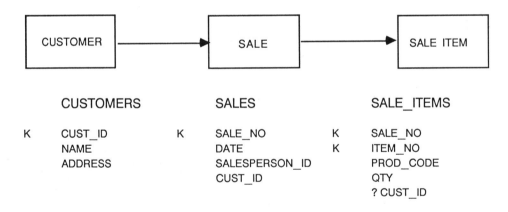

Should the CUSTOMER_ID be included, not only in the SALES table, but also in the SALE_ITEMS table?   It is not strictly necessary to do so, since if you want to know what customers have ordered a given product,   it's always possible to look up all the sale numbers in SALE_ITEMS for that product and then, using those sale numbers, to look up all the customers with those sale numbers in the SALES table.   But it may simplify programming to include the key of the grandparent entity (CUSTOMERS) in the child entity table (SALE_ITEMS).

5.4   Analyzing many-to-many relationships

As we noted in Chapter 1, a many-to-many relationship can always be resolved into two one-to-many relationships.   First, the keys to both entities must be identified, and then an "intersection entity" must be discovered or invented.

The key of the intersection entity is the combination or concatenation of the keys of the two original entities.   Take the case of the situation where one supplier supplies many products, and any one product may be supplied by several suppliers, as shown in the diagram below:

The single many-to-many line can be thought of as being made up of two one-to-many relationships, both ending on an intersection entity:

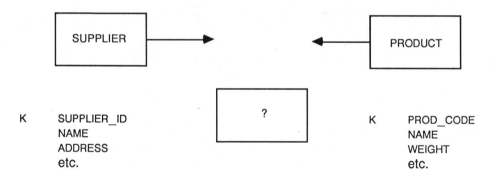

K	SUPPLIER_ID
	NAME
	ADDRESS
	etc.

K	PROD_CODE
	NAME
	WEIGHT
	etc.

K	SUPPLIER_ID
K	PROD_CODE
	PRICE_CHARGED
	DELIVERY_TIME
	etc.

We ask ourselves, "What entity is it that has a key which is the concatenation of a given supplier ID and a given product code?   What attributes depend uniquely on that combination?   What data elements can be determined if you know you are dealing with *this* product from *this* supplier?"

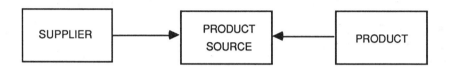

As before, we name this intersection entity, PRODUCT_SOURCE.   (We might equally   well   call   it   SUPPLIER_PRODUCT_OFFERING,   or SUPPLIER_QUOTATION.)   A given product may be available from different suppliers at different prices, and with different delivery times; a given supplier may offer many products.

This new entity will be represented in the eventual database by the table, PRODUCT_SOURCES.

```
Supplr ID Product Price Delivery
--------- ------- ----- --------
PER01     H134    6.95      10
HAV02     H134    6.50      14
PER01     T232    5.00       4
HAV02     T232    7.00       3
APP01     T232    7.00       4
```

Sometimes it's necessary to have a "key-only" or "non-information-bearing" intersection entity, just to express a many-to-many relationship.

5.5   Other notations used on E-R diagrams

Optional relationship

Conventionally a small open circle at the end of an association line indicates that there may be a relationship between any pair of instances of the associated entities, or there may not. A filled-in (black) circle indicates that there is always a relationship between any pair of instances of the entities. So this diagram:

should be read as

> "An employee <u>may be</u> assigned to one or more projects"
> "A project is (must be) staffed by one or more employees"

From the point of view of the structure of the relational database, this optionality makes no difference. Since the relationship is many-to-many, there will still be a table for EMPLOYEES, a table for PROJECTS, and a table describing the assignment of employees to projects (the intersection entity).

EMPLOYEES

PERSON_ID	FN	LN
26622	Robert	Brown
70904	Fred	Smith
04939	Rufus	Williams
17323	Ted	Bruce
.		

PROJECTS

PROJECT_ID	NAME
A179	Sales forecast
.	
C202	Back end study
.	
.	

PROJECT_
ASSIGNMENTS

PROJ_ID	PERSON_ID	ASSIGNED_ON
A179	70904	01-JUN-88
A179	17323	15-JUN-88
C202	04939	01-APR-88
.		

If an employee is *not* assigned to any project, as in the case of Robert Brown, there merely will be no row for him in the assignment table.

However, while optionality doesn't affect the structure of the database, it *does* affect the tests that have to be made to ensure referential integrity. If each project must have at least one employee, then if a new project is set up, and no employee is assigned to it, then the DBMS (or an application program) should send out an error message alerting the users to this lack of integrity.

Relationship to other instances of the same entity

In some circumstances, an entity can be related to itself.

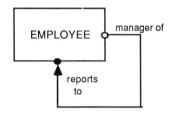

This diagram is to be read as:

"An employee may be manager of one or more other employees."
"An employee always reports to one and only one other employee."

This relationship would be implemented in the EMPLOYEES table thus:

```
EMPLOYEES

PERSON_ID    FN           LN           MANAGER
---------    ----------   ----------   -------
26622        Robert       Brown        04939
70904        Fred         Smith        04939
04939        Rufus        Williams     null
17323        Ted          Bruce        04939
  .                                      .
  .                                      .
```

Williams doesn't report to anybody; presumably he's the boss.

Either/or

Sometimes, it is necessary to show alternate possible relationships. This is conventionally done by placing an arc across the alternates:

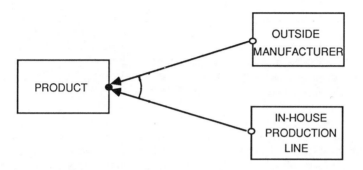

This diagram may be read as:

> "A product must be associated either with one outside manufacturer or with one in-house production-line."
> "An outside manufacturer may supply many products."
> "An in-house production-line may supply many products."

5.6   Time variance

For each entity, we should ask "Which of its attributes will change over time?". For each such attribute we should ask "Do we need to store the history of that attribute? If so, for how long a period of time or through how many changes?"

For example, if we consider a product, its price will probably change over time. Is it adequate to store merely the current price or should the history of the price of each product be kept available?   The size or color of the product may be changed.   Should the history of these attributes be kept or is it the case that when the size changes the product becomes a different product?   Do we need to keep records of discontinued products?

If we consider people or employees, what is the requirement to keep records of people who are no longer employed?   Is it possible for people to be rehired by the organization?   (In which case, a person may have two hire dates.)   Do we care about previous job titles?   Do we care about previous salaries?

Each time a decision is made to store the history of an attribute, a one-to-many relationship is implicitly set up, with a dependent table holding each change date and the value of the attribute from that date:

```
PEOPLE                                  SALARY_HISTORY

PERSON_ID  FN       LN        PERSON_ID  EFFECTIVE   SALARY
---------  -------  --------  ---------  ---------   ------
26622      Robert   Brown     26622      01-APR-85   22000
70904      Fred     Smith     70904      15-MAY-85   24500
.                             .
.                             26622      30-JUN-86   25000
.                             .
```

Once such a dependent table is created, the further question then arises whether the current value of the attribute, for example, CURRENT SALARY, should be stored in the main table, or whether it should be derived from the history table whenever it is needed.   This is really a performance issue, and will be discussed in Chapter 8.

As well as the issue of storing the history of various attribute values, we should consider how long records representing events, such as sales or purchases, need to be kept available in the system.   After 90 days, or six months, or seven years, (whatever is the appropriate value) each event record needs to be migrated to a history table for that type of event. It will either be purged altogether, and therefore lost to the system, (at least in machine-readable form), or be stored in such an archival form that it can be restored to the database, given certain notice, if it is required.

5.7 Sub-types and super-types of entities

One frequently finds that several entities discovered during E-R analysis are really different forms of the same entity. We mentioned the issue of former and present employees. Employees may also be paid hourly, daily or monthly, may or may not be on commission, and may or may not be eligible for overtime. But they are all people of interest to the system, with various classifications. It's important to recognize the similarities of entities where they exist. On an E-R diagram, these similarities may be shown by drawing boxes within boxes as shown below:

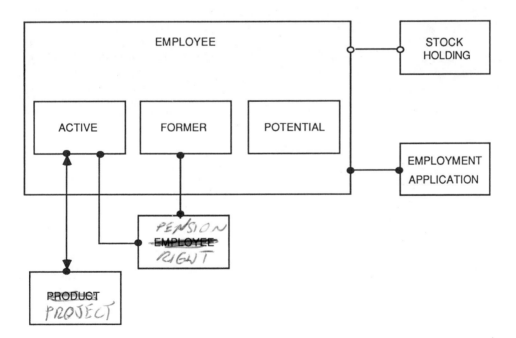

This diagram is to be read as saying that there are three sub-types of employees: active employees, former employees and potential employees. Only active employees are associated with projects. Any one active employee may be assigned to many projects. Any one project may have many active employees assigned to it.

Each active and former employee is associated with a pension right. Each pension right is associated with either an active employee or a former employee; potential employees (job applicants) have no pension rights (yet), since they have not earned anything yet.

Every employee must be associated with one employment application as the single line between the entity employment application and the super-type box "Employee" shows. Any one employee may be associated with a stockholding in the corporation.

The critical issue is how similar or different are the data elements which describe the various sub-groups. Can there be simply one table for all types of employees or must there be more than one table? The decision requires a careful weighing of the pros and cons in each case.

Consider the issue of employees and freelance consultants (who are not on staff but get paid on a daily basis). If records for both types of people are to be combined into one table, there needs to be a column denoting the status, perhaps "E" for Employee or "C" for Consultant giving a structure as shown here:

PERSON_ID	(is there any reason why consultants should not have a comparable ID?)
STATUS	E or C
NAME ETC	
COMPENSATION_PERIOD	Hour, day, month, year
COMPENSATION_PER_PERIOD	

The payroll and benefits programs will only process records where status equals "E".

Alternatively, the information can be held in two tables, as shown on the following page:

EMPLOYEES   CONSULTANTS

    EMPLOYEE_NO   CONSULTANT_ID
    NAME   NAME
    SALARY   FEE_PER_DAY

In this case, payroll will only process the employees table. However, now we have two tables, if we want to send a letter to all employees and consultants, sorted by zip code, we would need to combine both tables into a work table and sort the work table. Similarly, if both employees and consultants fill in timesheets, then the processing might well be more complex than if both types of people are stored in one table. The real issue is how often you want to look at the employees and consultants together, versus how often you need to look at them separately. If there is nothing to choose between having one or two tables, then, in general, it is better and simpler to have only one combined table.

To take another example, consider cash sales, sales paid for by check, credit card sales and billable sales. All sales have a date and a total amount. The type of sale can be stored in a column called HOW_PAID, with values:

CA - Cash   CC - Credit card   CK - Check   BI - Bill to client

So the structure of the table becomes as shown below:

Examples of values

SALE_DATE	5/1/89	5/1/89	5/1/89	5/1/89
TOTAL_AMOUNT	100	100	100	100
HOW_PAID	CA	CK	CC	BI
CHECK_NUMBER	null	9876	null	null
CREDIT_CARD_NUMBER	null	null	3714-2838	null
EXPIRATION_MONTH	null	null	12	null
EXPIRATION_YEAR	null	null	90	null
PURCHASE_ORDER_NUMBER	null	null	null	90501
PAYMENT_DATE	null	null	null	5/30/89

Given this structure, it follows that some elements will be null for every sale. For a cash sale, the credit card number will obviously be null, and so on. The significance of this depends on whether the DBMS allocates a fixed amount of space for a column, no matter whether it is null or not, or whether, (as in the case of ORACLE), null columns occupy no physical space on disk. Certainly, the programming effort involved in analyzing the totals of sales is much simpler in the case where there is only one table.

Of course, this table structure assumes that each sale stands on its own, and that billable sales are always paid in full. If a billable sale is, in fact, part of a continuing relationship with a client, where several invoices may be outstanding at any one time, and partial payments, or overpayments, may be received, then this simple one-table structure will no longer be adequate.

5.8 The end result of E-R analysis

Once all the issues discussed in this chapter have been resolved, you should have an E-R diagram in which each box can be represented as a table (or set of related tables) in the eventual database for the system. All one-to-one relationships should have been examined and determined to be non-collapsible. The pointers that will establish each relationship should have been defined. No many-to-many relationships should appear; they should all have been resolved into one-to-many relationships.

Many of the available CASE tools support the drawing and changing of E-R diagrams, as discussed in Appendix A.

References

5-1   Sweet, F. *Building Database Applications.*
       Jacksonville, FL: Boxes & Arrows Publishing, 1986

5-2   Curtice, R. M. and Jones, P. E. *Logical Data Base Design.*
       Wellesley, MA: QED, 1987

5-3   Howe, D. R. *Data Analysis for Data Base Design.*
       Baltimore: Arnold, 1983

Exercises and discussion points:

1.   Draw an entity-relationship diagram for the system which you chose as the basis for developing a data flow diagram in Chapter 4, Exercise 1.

       Resolve the 1:1 and 1:many relationships, using the guidelines given in this chapter. What did you learn about the structure of the data stores?

2.   Suppose employees may also be customers, and get employee discounts. How would you reflect that fact on an E-R diagram? What would be the consequences for the structure of the database?

Chapter 6

Logical modelling: detailed data definition

In the two preceding chapters, we discussed the use of a data flow diagram for defining the scope of a proposed information system and the use of an entity-relationship diagram for clarifying the nature of the data stores on a diagram.

Depending on the nature of a project, at this point in the logical modelling process you may know a lot or a little about the details of the contents of the data stores. For example, if your system will use a customer table which already exists, you will know exactly what data elements it contains. On the other hand, if the new system is to capture information about, say, industry financial data (which has never been defined before), you may have only the vaguest idea of the details.

You may have noted in the previous chapter that, in order to do entity-relationship analysis, we had to ask quite a number of detailed questions about the key identifiers of an entity, what attributes varied with time, and so on.

The next step in logical modelling, therefore, is to define the exact contents of each data store. This is done by defining, as simply as possible, the data elements that will need to be held to describe the attributes of each entity on the E-R diagram, and then deciding whether each table should be in a data store alone, or whether there are two or more tables which will be accessed together so frequently that it is meaningful to put them in the same data store.

6.1 Three approaches to deciding what to store in the database

Where you are not clear on the details of the data elements that need to be held about each entity, there are three approaches that can be taken:

Approach 1: Common minimum

In this approach, one takes the inputs and/or outputs that one has most information about, and works forward from the inputs, or backward from the outputs, to each data store. The aim is to work out the smallest number of data elements which will be sufficient to derive the outputs or capture the essence of the inputs.

To take a very simplified example, the figure shows an output of "Sales reports." The sample lists the units and the dollar volume for each product in each region, both for today and month-to-date:

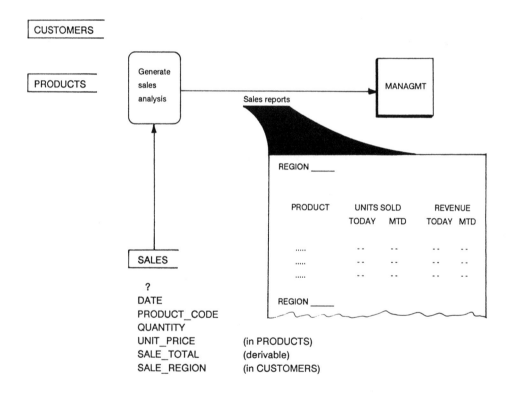

On the face of it, the data elements required to produce the sales report are the sale region, the date of each sale, the product code, the quantity of each product sold, and the unit price at which it was sold, from which the sale total can be derived.

Will these all be stored in the sales table? No: the unit price is an attribute of the product, while the sale region is an attribute of the customer to whom the product was sold. So only DATE, PRODUCT_CODE, QUANTITY and CUST_ID need be stored in the sales table, at least as far as this particular output is concerned.

Conversely, one might take an input describing a sale which holds the date, the time of day, the day of the week, the customer name, the product name and the quantity ordered.

A similar process of reduction should be carried out. If the date is stored, the day of the week is redundant since it can be computed. If the time of day is not used in any known output required from the system, is it worth storing? (This is a question for the users to resolve, with an eye to outputs that may be required in the future.) If the CUST_ID and PRODUCT_CODE can be retrieved given the customer names and product names, then the names need not be stored, at least not in the SALES table.

This approach yields a lot of detailed information, but it tends not to discover every data element which is needed, principally because it's hard for users of a system to imagine, in advance, every possible output they will ever want.

Approach 2: Analysis by wandering about

The second approach is to visit the places where the business is conducted, to examine the objects (such as products), study the events (such as sales), and note the attributes that they have which will be of interest to the business.

Every object usually has a unique identifier; also, usually one needs to store its name, together with what it costs, and perhaps what it is sold for. Heavy objects, like machines, have a recordable location, and a capacity (for example, widgets per second). Light objects, like hammers, are commonly issued to some person who is responsible for them. Almost all objects have a date of acquisition (hiring in the case of a person), and a date of disposal (termination); there may be other dates used to describe the object's life-cycle, such as the dates a machine is overhauled, or the dates a person is promoted.

Every event must be given a unique identifier; it almost always has a date (and possibly a time) of occurrence, and often two or more associated objects (such as a customer ordering a product or a person being assigned to a project).

This approach tends to cast its net too wide, and to discover too much, but it is a corrective to Approach 1. It does encourage the analyst to get direct exposure to the business, rather than simply relying on the user's statements.

Approach 3: If it were my business

The third approach may be described as using empathy. If *you* ran this business, what would *you* want to have stored in the system? Obviously, the more you know about the business and understand the users' objective in setting up the system, the more valuable the results of Approach 3 will be.

This approach is sometimes attacked as being arrogant. How dare a systems analyst tell a business person how the business should be run? This attack is misconceived: as an analyst you should not *dictate* the nature of the system, but it is entirely helpful for you to offer *suggestions*. It is in general easier for a user to be offered a list, and to be asked what additions and deletions are needed, than to be asked to compose the same list from scratch. So you are doing the user a service in saying "From my limited knowledge of the business, it seems that it would be useful to have the following pieces of information stored in the system. Is there anything I've missed? Bearing in mind that information costs money to capture and store, is there anything on this list that you really don't value much?"

By pooling the results of the three approaches, it's always possible to produce a draft definition of the contents of each data store and each table describing an entity.

In addition, existing data dictionaries should be consulted, to see if any other relevant data elements have been defined already. For example, if you are defining a system and you decide that you will need to store data about customers and products, it is possible that the data administration group in your organization has already defined many data elements describing these entities, so that you can capitalize on this work and avoid reinventing the wheel.

6.2   Data element naming and description

Each data element should have a unique name which should be as meaningful as possible without being inconveniently long.   Especially if the nature of the data is not evident from the name, it is very convenient, during analysis, to have a description of each data element which fully explains the nature of the data itself.   This description may be stored in a data dictionary for easy access.

There are many approaches and conventions that have been proposed for data naming.   The approach recommended in this book is that the description of the data element should be in the form *"noun + of/which is + qualifier"* and the name should normally be in the form *"qualifier + noun."*

Thus, a data element which would be described as "the quantity of a product which is the total on-order at any given time," or some such, would be given the name "ON_ORDER_QUANTITY."

A data element which would be described as "the date of actual shipment of a consignment   from   our   premises,"   would   be   given   the   name, "ACTUAL_SHIPPING_DATE."

Description	Name	Abbreviated name
noun + of/which is + qualifier ...	qualifier + noun	
Quantity of a product which is on-order	ON_ORDER_ QUANTITY	ON_ORD_QTY
Date of actual shipment	ACTUAL_SHIPPING_ DATE	ACT_SHPG_DTE

One reason for adopting this format of the physical name is that, often, report generators use the physical element name as the heading of a column on a report and truncate the name to the default width of the column.   The "qualifier + noun" format preserves the most meaning in such a circumstance, as the two examples below will show:

Data name	Truncated to 6 characters
QUANTITY_ON_ORDER	QUANTI
QUANTITY_IN_STOCK	QUANTI
ON_ORDER_QUANTITY	ON_ORD
IN_STOCK_QUANTITY	IN_STO

Partly for this reason, and also to save keystrokes, it's usually a good idea to have a set of minimum standard abbreviations for data names. A suggested list is given here; of course, many installations have their own list.

ACTUAL	ACT
ADDRESS	ADDR
AMOUNT	AMT
AREA	AREA
BALANCE	BAL
BILLING	BLLG
CODE	CODE
CREDIT	CR
CURRENT	CURR
CUSTOMER	CUS
DATE	DTE
DEBIT	DR
DELIVERY	DELY
FIRST NAME	FN
IDENTIFIER	ID
INVENTORY	INVY
INVOICE	INVC
LAST NAME	LN
MIDDLE INITIAL	MI
MONTH	MTH
MONTH TO DATE	MTHTD
MONTHLY	MTHLY
NUMBER	NO
ORDER	ORD
OUTSTANDING	OS
PAYMENT	PAYT
PERSON	PER
PHONE	PHONE
PREVIOUS	PREV
PRODUCT	PROD
PROJECT	PROJ
PROJECTED	PROJD
PURCHASE	PUR
QUANTITY	QTY
QUARTER	QR
QUARTER TO DATE	QRTD
REGION	REGN
SALARY	SALRY
SALE	SALE
SALESMAN	SMAN
SHIPPING	SHPG
STATE	ST
STOCK	STK
STREET	STREET
SUPPLIER	SUP
UNITS	UTS
WEEKLY	WKLY
YEAR	YR
YEAR TO DATE	YRTD

Synonyms or aliases

In many cases, one finds that different names are used for the same entity in different parts of an organization. The terms "employee," "member of staff," "MOS," "personnel-cost-line-item," might be used in different systems departments to mean a person who works for the organization. These are synonyms, multiple names meaning the same underlying thing.

Name	Thing
Employee Personnel-cost-line-item Member of staff MOS	

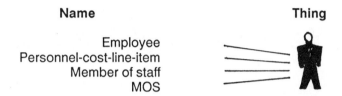

While it's better that synonyms should be avoided, they can be coped with by choosing one name to be the principal name and describing the others as the synonym or alias for that principal name.

Homonyms

The converse situation exists where a given term can mean more than one thing or entity. A classical example is that of a projected delivery date. This seems a simple enough concept; the only problem with it is, where exactly is the delivery projected to take place? When the ship arrives in the harbor? When the goods are on the dock? When the goods are in the customs shed? When the goods have been cleared with customs? When the goods are actually delivered to our factory?

Name	Thing
Projected delivery date	Date that ship arrives in harbor Date that goods are released from customs Date that goods are in ready-use store

Take, again, the innocent looking term, PRICE. Does this mean selling price, cost price, bulk price, discounted price?

Such "homonyms" (where one word means more than one thing) are often hard to spot, because people in different departments can use the same terms, (like "projected delivery date") amongst their own limited working group without any ambiguity.

In the Traffic Department, "projected-delivery-date" might mean the day the ship arrives in the harbor; in the Customs Brokering Department it might mean the day the goods are released from customs; in Production Control it might mean the day the goods are available, unpacked and checked, in the ready-use store. Within each small group no problem arises, because the term means only one thing: it's only when the analyst tries to create a system which crosses departmental boundaries that problems may arise unless the different meanings of the homonym are detected and dealt with.

The important issue is whether it will be completely clear, from the context in which the homonym is used, which of the various possible meanings it is to have. If it's not completely clear from the context, then each separate thing must be given a different name.

Naming the element after its domain

The domain of a data element is the set of all eligible values for that element. Thus the domain of a date might be any valid date later than January 1st, 1900. The domain of a temperature might be any value from $-273°$ to $5000°$. If you know that a data element has a certain domain, you know the basic editing criteria for acceptable values (though not the rules for comparing one data element with another, such as that the hiring date must be earlier than the firing date). For this reason every domain should have a standard name, and where a data element belongs to a shared domain, its name should contain that domain's name, qualified if necessary.

So all dates should end in _DTE, and all salaries end in _SALRY (not some _SAL and others _SALARY). Where no possibility of a homonym arises, the domain name alone can be used. Thus, in the CUSTOMER table, ZIP (the domain name) can be used unqualified, likewise in the EMPLOYEE table, and in the SUPPLIERS table. No possibility of confusion exists.

Attributes of the domain and attributes of the data element

The name and one-sentence description of a data element are the basic facts about it, but for analysis to be complete, several other attributes of each data element need to be defined. Some of these attributes will be shared by every data element that belongs to a given domain: some attributes belong to only one particular data element.

Attributes shared by all data elements in a domain include:

1. Data type, meaning whether numeric or string, plus length and format, if any. The exact data types which data elements may be given vary from DBMS to DBMS. Some DBMSs allow numeric domains to be integer, small integer, decimal, or floating point, and allow string domains to contain any character, or only letters, and to be a normal length (for example, up to 255 characters long) or to be very long (for example, up to 4,096 characters long), which carries some restrictions on usage. Some DBMSs support a DATE data type.

2. Domain type, meaning whether the eligible values are defined by being on a list (a discrete domain, such as state-code), or by satisfying some rule (a continuous domain, such as salary or temperature). For a discrete domain, the eligible values need to be listed in a convenient table, together with the meaning of each value (since usually the meanings are used in the system). For a continuous domain, the defining rule has to be specified, giving the highest and lowest acceptable values, where relevant.

3. One or more examples of an eligible value may be worth documenting. Rather than ask the users to specify the length of a field, it may be easier to ask for the largest/longest example the user can imagine. Could anyone have a salary over $1 million? What's the longest first name we should handle?

So a discrete domain might be defined as follows:

Domain name:	CITIZEN_STATUS
Data type:	ALPHA length 1
Discrete or Continuous:	Discrete
Table of values/meanings:	CITIZEN_STATUS_MEANINGS
Contents:	Value Meaning

Value	Meaning
C	US Citizen by birth
N	US Citizen by naturalization
R	Permanent resident with green card
A	Illegal alien, eligible for amnesty
I	Illegal alien, not eligible for amnesty
V	Visitor or other non-resident alien.

A continuous domain might be defined as:

Domain name:	PERSON_WEIGHT
Data type:	INTEGER length 3
Discrete or continuous:	Continuous
High limit:	500
Low limit:	80
Other parts of defining rule:	Weight in pounds wearing underwear only, rounded to nearest pound.

Attributes which are specific to a given data element (once you know its domain) are:

1. The name of *this* data element. For instance, there might be several elements called APPLICANT_CITIZEN_STATUS, STOCKHOLDER_ CITIZEN_STATUS, CUSTOMER_CONTACT_CITIZEN_STATUS, and so on, all of which share the domain CITIZEN_STATUS.

2. The description of *this* data element. Each of the data elements above will have a slightly different description, though all share the same domain.

3. Whether the data element is captured from outside the system, originated within the system, or derivable from other data elements. A captured data element must appear in some input dialogue or other interface; an originated data element (for example, a transaction identifier which is incremented by the system) must have the originating method specified; a derivable data element such as ITEM_TOTAL (derived from QTY * UNIT_PRICE) must have its derivation rule specified.

4. The ownership of the data element, meaning the person or business unit responsible for its correctness, who has the final authority over whether the data element has been inserted or updated correctly. For example, the VP of Sales may own the data element SELLING_PRICE, in the sense that only he can authorize a change in the value of SELLING_PRICE for any product.

6.3 Key (identifier) fields

Once the data elements which will be the columns in a table have been defined and named, one or more columns must be chosen to be the key or identifier, in such a way that once you know the value of the key, you can pick out one and only one row from the table. To put it another way, the key uniquely identifies each row in the table.

If there is no unique identifier in a table, we cannot refer to that table and be sure that we are picking out the row that we want. At the simplest, if employees are not identified in the EMPLOYEES table other than by first name and last name, then putting JOHN SMITH as a value of MANAGER in the table that describes DEPARTMENTS is risky. The reference to the EMPLOYEES table will only work so long as there is only one John Smith, and so long as Mr. Smith doesn't change his name. (Or, if he does change it, we must be sure to change the stored value *everywhere* it occurs in the database).

So a key must be unique now and always, and once assigned, must never change. Further, it must never have a missing or null value, because if it does, it may not be unique and certainly cannot be used as a cross-reference pointer.

If a key cannot be found from the data elements which "naturally" describe each entity, then a unique identifier (such as EMPLOYEE_NO) must be created. This is a "dataless" or "arbitrary" key, assigned perhaps by the system incrementing a number for each new employee, which is stored *only* to provide a unique key.

Some writers have gone so far as to recommend that a system-assigned dataless key be used for all entities: this book does not go so far, provided the key chosen will always be unique and will not change once assigned.

Consider an interesting borderline case. A system identifies each sale with the field SALE_NO, whose format is YMMDDnn. Thus the first sale on Jan 1st, 1988 receives a SALE_NO of 8010101, and the 99th sale on Dec 31st, 1988 gets 8123199. Will this key always be unique? Only if ten years is "always," since both numbers may repeat in 1998. Of course, in many applications this is adequate. Will this key ever be changed? Only if the users agree that they will never want to backdate a sale, or to hold it in the system "as-of" some date other than the one it actually took place.

Perhaps the worst risk is that one day there will be more than 100 sales. While an occasional flood of sales could be handled by the "white lie" of assigning tomorrow's date to sales in excess of 100, a steady flow of more than 100 a day would mean that the key would need to be extended.

But provided the risks are understood by responsible users, and are acceptable, you could combine 2 columns into one in this way.

The alternative would be to have an arbitrary system-incremented sale number, and hold SALE_DTE as a separate column. Assuming there are less than 100 sales per day, a 5-digit sale number will not repeat for at least 4 years. Is 4 years "always?" In other words, is it satisfactory for this system to have a key where a sale made in 1993 may have the same identifier as a sale in 1988? If not, a 6-digit number would not repeat for at least 40 years.

Embedded structures

Particularly where keys have been inherited from older manual systems, one should watch out for the possibility that different parts of the key have special meanings. For instance, every book is assigned a unique 10-digit International Standard Book Number (ISBN), which has the format:

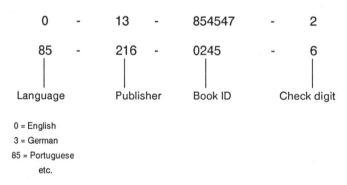

It may be desirable for the fields embedded in a common structure like this to be stored in separate columns, so that one could, for example, sort all the books in a table by publisher's code.

Multiple candidates for key

Sometimes, there is more than one column, or group of columns, that will uniquely identify each row in a table. For example, in an EMPLOYEES table, not only will EMPLOYEE_NO be a unique identifier (by definition), but also SOCIAL_SECURITY_NO may serve to identify each employee. Even in a large organization, there may well be no Smiths born in New York on the same day, so LAST_NAME combined with DATE_OF_BIRTH and PLACE_OF_BIRTH could conceivably be a key.

Why choose one candidate key over another? First, do we believe that a candidate, even if unique now, will always be unique? Secondly, can a candidate ever be null? Thirdly, will a candidate ever change?

The answers to the first and third questions go against LAST_NAME + DATE_OF_BIRTH + PLACE_OF_BIRTH since though the concatenated value may be unique in fact, it is not unique in principle, and as we have noted, LAST_NAME may change. The answer to the second question goes against SOCIAL_SECURITY_NUMBER, since we may employ people before we know what their SSN is, or may employ foreigners, who do not have an SSN.

The decision between candidates cannot always be resolved by these questions. Take a table of STATE_CODE, STATE_NAME and POPULATION. While POPULATION will change, STATE_CODE and STATE_NAME are both unique and unchanging non-null identifiers. The choice comes down to one of convenience. Where a cross-reference is to be maintained in other tables, the code is much terser and less liable to mis-spelling than the state-name.

6.4 Simplifying tables through normalization

As we noted in Chapter 1, in database discussions the word "relation" means a table of data; so a relational database is one made up of a group of linked tables.

The term "relation" derives from the study of data made by E. F. (Ted) Codd and others, then at IBM, trying to think out a theoretically sound way of describing data that would lead to the design of flexible, changeable data structures (Ref 6-1). In thinking about data, Codd found the mathematics of sets to be helpful. A mathematical set may be thought of as a group of objects with an associated defining rule or list that enables you to tell whether a given object is in the set or not. Thus, the set of all even numbers is a subset of the set of all numbers with the defining rule that each member is exactly divisible by 2. The set of white rabbits is a subset of the set of all rabbits with the defining property that the animal has white fur all over, and so on.

Any given data value may be thought of as a member of the set of all possible values for that data element; thus the state-code "NY" is a member of the set of all valid state-codes. As we noted earlier, the set of all eligible values for a data element is called its "domain," usually defined either by a list or by upper and lower bounds. The domain of SALARY might be any number with 2 decimal places between 4999.99 and 100000.00; the domain of AIRPORT_CODE is a list of 3-letter groups like JFK, LAX and so on.

If one has several domains defined, it is possible to make another set by taking a value from domain 1, a value from domain 2, and so on. By analogy with words like "quintuple" and "octuple" such a set is called a "tuple." A tuple with values from each of 2 domains (for example, CA, California) is a 2-tuple, from 3 domains a 3-tuple, and so on. If one had a set of 2-tuples such that for every member of the domain STATE_CODE there was a corresponding member of the domain STATE_NAME, one would have a table of state-code meanings. For this set of tuples to be useful, you would need to know what each domain signified (translation: the table would have to have headings). So we come to the formal definition of a relation, "A set of domain-names plus a set of tuples, where each tuple consists of a set of name-value pairs, one pair for each domain, where the value is drawn from the domain of that name."

The STATE_CODE/STATE_NAME relation can be written out:

```
( STATE CODE : CA      )   ( STATE NAME : California )
( STATE CODE : FL      )   ( STATE NAME : Florida    )
( STATE CODE : AK      )   ( STATE NAME : Alaska     )
.
.
.
```

Note that there is nothing in this definition about the sequence of the tuples, and that's something to bear in mind when we show the relation in the more familiar form of a table:

```
STATE CODE  STATE NAME             STATE NAME  STATE CODE
----------  ----------             ----------  ----------
CA          California             Florida     FL
FL          Florida                New Jersey  NJ
AK          Alaska                 California  CA
NJ          New Jersey             Alaska      AK
.
.
```

From the relational point of view, both these tables are identical; the sequence left to right, or from top to bottom, means nothing and holds no information about the data. So when we say that a relation is a table, it is a table with this special nature. Part of the flexibility of a relational database comes from this property; no information is "hidden" in the physical layout of the database.

To summarize this terminology:

Set-theory	Relational database	Conventional DP
Relation	Table	File
Domain	All the possible values a column can have	All the possible values a field can have
Tuple	Row	Record

In a mathematical set, no duplicates of any object are allowed. Since a relation is a set of tuples, in theory no row in a relation can be a duplicate of any other row. (In practice, SQL allows you to have duplicate rows in a table, though there are ways of eliminating them if you want to.) As we noted in the previous section, if a column or concatenation of columns can not be found to uniquely identify each row, then a special key column must be invented.

Normalization of relations (simplification of tables)

Some tables are easier to change than others. Considerable attention has been given to tests for ease of changeability; five types of table, called in the jargon "normalized forms," have been identified.

First normal form refers to any table which has only one value per cell, or row/column intersection. The table:

```
Part #      Depots at which stored
------      ----------------------
T232        Chicago,  Denver,  Orlando
H995        Denver,  Chicago
  .
```

is not in any normal form; it is unnormalized. However, the table:

Part #	Depot	In stock qty	Depot phone	No. of boxes
T232	Chicago	467	312/222-9876	47
T232	Denver	319	313/675-9786	32
T232	Orlando	121	305/745-0934	13
H995	Denver	578	313/675-9786	58
H995	Chicago	227	312/222-9876	23
.				
.				

is in first normal form.

Second normal form

To test whether a table is in second normal form, we ask:

1) What is the key to this relation?

   If the key is concatenated (more than one column), we then also ask:

2) Are there any non-key columns which depend on only part of the key?

For the table at the bottom of the previous page, what is the key? Clearly, "Part #" alone is not enough to uniquely identify a given row; we need to concatenate "Depot" with "Part #" to get a unique key.

Since the key is concatenated, we also ask the second question.

Does "In stock qty" depend on only part of the key? No, you have to know both the Part # and the Depot.

Does "Depot phone" depend on only part of the key? Yes; if you know the Depot you know its phone, without caring about the Part #.

The table above is therefore not in second normal form, since it does not pass the test:

> *A first normal form table is also in second normal form if every non-key column depends on the whole of the key.*

What is wrong with having a table in first normal form?

1) The database will take up more room on disk than it need do, since the phone number is repeated for every part stored in the same depot.

2) If a depot changes its phone number, the change must be made to every row for a part in that depot.

3) If anything goes wrong with the updating process, a depot may appear to have different phone numbers depending on which row is retrieved later on; the integrity of the database will be lost.

4) If the whole row for a part is deleted when the part is not stored in a given depot, there may be nowhere in the database to store the phone number of a depot, just because it happens to be empty for the time being.

To avoid these disadvantages, the table above must be split into 2 tables:

PART_STORAGE

Part #	Depot	In stock qty	No. of boxes
T232	Chicago	467	47
T232	Denver	319	32
T232	Orlando	121	13
H995	Denver	578	58
H995	Chicago	227	23
.			
.			

DEPOT_DATA

Depot	Depot phone
Chicago	312/222-9876
Denver	313/675-9786
Orlando	305/745-0934
.	
.	

Both of these tables are in second normal form (2NF for short). The top table, PART_STORAGE, is in 2NF because both the non-key columns ("In stock qty" and "Number of containers") are dependent on the concatenated key, the whole concatenated key, and nothing but the concatenated key. The second table, DEPOT_DATA, is automatically in 2NF because it does not have a concatenated key, and so the non-key column "Depot phone" must naturally be dependent on the whole of the single key column "Depot."

Looked at another way, the 1NF table is holding facts which describe 2 separate things: the storage of parts, and the depot in which they are stored. As a general rule, one table in a database should describe only one entity; it should contain facts about only one thing or class of things.

Third normal form (3NF)

To test whether a 2NF table is also in 3NF, we ask: Are any of the non-key columns dependent on any other non-key columns? PART_STORAGE has 2 non-key columns. If you know a value for "In stock qty" do you then know the corresponding value for "Number of boxes?" Well, yes, you do; the table shows that all parts are packed in boxes of 10, so the number of boxes can be derived from the quantity by dividing by 10 and rounding up to cover partly-empty boxes. So there is a dependency between the two non-key columns created by this "business rule," and PART_STORAGE is not in 3NF, though it can be made so by removing "Number of boxes," saving space and possible loss of integrity. (If the business rule were different, and each individual box held a different number of parts, then the number of boxes would be an independent fact, and PART_STORAGE would be in 3NF as it stands above.) The rule is:

A second normal form table is also in third normal form if no non-key column depends on any other non-key column.

Another common case met with in normalization arises with a table like:

```
EMPLOYEE_NO      DEPARTMENT      BUILDING
-----------      ----------      --------
26622            Sales           West block
41156            Accounts        Headquarters
33987            Research        North Lab
88644            Sales           West block
```

This table is in 1NF; it does not have a concatenated key since EMPLOYEE_NO uniquely identifies each row, so it is automatically in 2NF. Is there a dependency between the non-key columns? Well, it depends. If it is the case that a department is housed in only one building, then if you know the department, you know the building, so the table is not in 3NF, and should be split into:

```
EMPLOYEE_NO   DEPARTMENT    and    DEPARTMENT   BUILDING
```

If, on the other hand, employees work all over, wherever space can be found, then the building is a fact about an employee, not about a department, and the table above *is* in 3NF.

This brings up the issue of changeability of table design.   What would happen if the business changed three months after the system was implemented, so that whereas previously each department was in a given building, now employees work all over?   The two-table design will now not hold the necessary facts, and the database will have to be restructured, back to the one-table design.

Consequently,   if the designer suspects that the present business situation might change, it would be prudent to implement the one-table design, which is more changeable, even though it is initially only in 2NF and involves redundant information (at present).

Note how simplification of data requires knowledge of the business, of the "business rules" which set up relationships between data elements, and of possible changes in those business rules.

Fourth normal form (4NF)

As a general rule, 3NF tables are easy to understand, easy to update, and easy to retrieve data from.   Occasionally, though, a problem arises if a given non-key column can have multiple values for a given key value.   Consider:

```
FACULTY_MEMBER        COURSE_TAUGHT           DEGREE
--------------        -------------           ------
Poindexter            Biology 101             AB
Poindexter            Statistics 703          BS
Poindexter                                    MA
Poindexter                                    PhD
Farthingale           Statistics 703          AB
Farthingale           Poetry 666
Farthingale           Relativity 900
```

What is the key for this table?   FACULTY_MEMBER is not a unique identifier, neither is the concatenation of FACULTY_MEMBER and COURSE_TAUGHT, as the third and fourth rows show, neither is the concatenation of FACULTY_MEMBER and DEGREE.   We are forced to conclude that the key is the concatenation of all three columns.   Since there are no non-key columns, the table must be in 2NF and in 3NF, passing both tests.   It still has a problem though.   If Poindexter is assigned 3 more classes, how will the table be updated?   Will 3 more rows be inserted with null DEGREEs, or will existing null slots be filled up and then another row inserted, or what?   This table fails the test for 4NF:

A third normal form table is also in fourth normal form if it does not contain more than one multi-valued fact about the entity described by the table.

The table is trying to hold 2 multi-valued facts: the various courses taught and the degrees held. Even though it is in 3NF, holding more than one multi-valued fact makes it hard to update.

The table needs to be split into 2 tables, both of which are now in 4NF.

```
FACULTY_MEMBER COURSE_TAUGHT
-------------- -------------
Poindexter     Biology 101
Poindexter     Statistics 703
Farthingale    Statistics 703
Farthingale    Poetry 666
Farthingale    Relativity 900


FACULTY_MEMBER DEGREE
-------------- ------
Poindexter     AB
Poindexter     BS
Poindexter     MA
Poindexter     PhD
Farthingale    AB
```

If now Poindexter is given 3 more classes, or Farthingale gets her PhD, the update procedure is quite clear and simple.

Fifth normal form (5NF)

In some even rarer instances, it may be simpler to split a 4NF relation up into 2 or more tables.

A fourth normal form relation is in fifth normal form when its information content cannot be reconstructed from several smaller relations, not having the same key.

For a discussion of 5NF, see Reference 6-2.

6.5   Code-interpretation tables

As you can see from the previous section, the process of normalization results in the production of numerous tables. A good proportion of the tables that result, however, have only two columns: a code of some kind, and the meanings to be attached to this code.

Consider the table:

```
FLT_NO DEPARTS FROM_AIRPORT      CODE TO_AIRPORT         CODE
------ ------- ----------------  ---- -----------------  ----
996    1230    San Francisco     SFO  New York-Kennedy   JFK
 .
 .
 .
```

This cannot be in third normal form because there is a dependency between non-key fields: if you know a code, you know the airport name and vice versa. The table should be broken into two:

ROUTINGS

```
FLIGHT_NO DEPARTS FROM_CODE TO_CODE
--------- ------- --------- --------
996       1230    SFO       JFK
 .
 .
 .
```

AIRPORT_CODES

```
CODE AIRPORT_NAME
---- ----------------
DFW  Dallas-Fort Worth
JFK  New York-Kennedy
SFO  San Francisco
 .
 .
```

Two-column tables like AIRPORT_CODES will be referred to as "code-interpretation" tables. They typically hold data that is relatively stable (airport codes and state codes are very rarely changed, and a marital status of M will mean "MARRIED" for a long time to come). Their significance will be discussed in Chapter 8.

6.6 Redrafting the data flow diagram

As we saw in Chapter 1, the DFD may need to be redrafted after the data has been defined and the contents of the data stores simplified to 4NF tables.

While each table *could* be made into a single data store, it makes for greater clarity to:

a)   omit code-interpretation tables from the DFD (though keeping them in the data model).

b)   group in a single data store any tables which are usually accessed together because they describe the same entity (like SALES and SALES_ITEMS).

References

6-1   Codd, E.F.   *A relational model of data for large shared data banks.* Communications of the ACM, June 1970.

6-2   Kent, W.   *A simple guide to five normal forms in relational database theory.* Communications of the ACM, February 1983.

6-3   Date, C.   *Relational Database: selected writings.*   Addison-Wesley, 1984.

Exercises and discussion points:

1.   Consider the monthly statement that you receive from your bank. What data elements are represented on it? What is the minimum information that your bank must hold about your account(s) in order to generate this statement? From what inputs is the information derived? Do all the data elements in these inputs end up on your statement? If not, which ones are missing?

2.   "Wander about" a modern automobile. How many data elements of interest concerning it can you identify in 5 minutes? (50 is a good number.)

3.   Review your own organization's data naming and abbreviation conventions. Are there any ways in which it is better than the convention described in this chapter?

4.   Review the data elements in a system with which you are familiar. How many of them share a domain? How many of them belong to domains where they are the only data elements?

5.   What embedded structures are in use in your organization?

6.   Some analysts recommend assigning an arbitrary, meaningless key to every table. What are the arguments for and against this?

7.   In the light of your answer to Exercise 1, develop the 4NF tables that your bank would need to hold in order to produce your bank statement.

Chapter 7

Table processing operations

Given that a database can be made out of normalized tables, we need a standard set of commands for defining the tables, storing data in them, and retrieving that data in various ways.

There are several languages that have been developed for doing this. The American National Standard "for the functionality of the interfaces ... to a relational database management system" is SQL (Structured Query Language), so in this discussion we will use the SQL commands.

7.1 Creating tables

Suppose you want to set up this table, holding the data shown:

```
CODE    ITEM          DESCRIPTION        PRICE
----    ------------  ----------------   ------

T134    Spanner       Adjustable         11.99
T135    Spanner       9/16 inch           7.25
T114    Spanner       7/16 inch           4.89
T232    Wrench        Adjustable         13.55
T177    Pliers        Long nose           8.19
T179    Pliers        Electrical          9.95
```

You first need to enter an SQL command to create the necessary definition of the table, then you need to enter commands to insert the data. To create the table definition, you have to supply a name for the table, then name each column and give the type of data to be stored in it, with the maximum size to be allowed. For the table above, the CREATE TABLE statement might be as follows:

CREATE TABLE PRODUCTS . . .	The name you are giving the table is "PRODUCTS"
(CODE CHAR(4) NOT NULL, . . .	Since CODE is the key identifier, you don't want it
	ever to be missing: defining it as NOT NULL
	means that a value must be provided for every row
ITEM CHAR(12), . . .	Note each column and datatype is separated
DESCRIPTION CHAR(15),	by a comma
PRICE NUMBER(5,2)); . . .	This means 5 positions in all, with 2 decimal places

The "data types," which you can use, such as CHAR(15), vary somewhat from DBMS to DBMS.

For instance, IBM's DB2 would use: **PRICE DECIMAL (5,2)**

Once the table is created, you would enter

INSERT INTO PRODUCTS VALUES (' T134 ' , ' Spanner ' , ' Adjustable ', 11.99) ;

and this would set up the first row in the table. In principle, you need to enter each row with a separate statement; in practice, you would set up a screen application which would allow you to enter the column values on the screen, and which would then generate a series of INSERT statements when you pressed the "Execute" key.

Once the data has been loaded into the table, entering

SELECT * FROM PRODUCTS;   (* means "all")

will display (or print, or both):

```
CODE ITEM          DESCRIPTION        PRICE
---- ------------  ----------------   ------

T134 Spanner       Adjustable         11.99
T135 Spanner       9/16 inch           7.25
T114 Spanner       7/16 inch           4.89
T232 Wrench        Adjustable         13.55
T177 Pliers        Long nose           8.19
T179 Pliers        Electrical          9.95
```

Unless you specify otherwise, the column headings and widths are the same as the names and widths you supplied in the CREATE statement, the rows are listed in the order they were inserted, the columns are listed in the order they were defined in the CREATE statement, and one space is provided between each column.

7.2 Selecting certain columns (projection)

If, instead of asking for "all columns" with the *, you name only the columns you want to see, thus:

SELECT ITEM, DESCRIPTION FROM PRODUCTS;

you will get:

```
ITEM            DESCRIPTION
------------    --------------

Spanner         Adjustable
Spanner         9/16 inch
Spanner         7/16 inch
Wrench          Adjustable
Pliers          Long nose
Pliers          Electrical
```

This type of operation, where a new table is made by extracting columns from the original table and sticking them together, is referred to as "projection."

7.3 Selecting only certain rows (selection)

If you wanted to know what was available for less than $5, you would enter:

SELECT * FROM PRODUCTS WHERE PRICE < 5;

which would give:

```
CODE ITEM         DESCRIPTION        PRICE
---- ------------ ---------------- ------

T114 Spanner      7/16 inch            4.89
```

The "WHERE clause" can involve a character comparison:

SELECT * FROM PRODUCTS WHERE DESCRIPTION = ' Adjustable ' ;

which will give:

```
CODE ITEM         DESCRIPTION        PRICE
---- ------------ ---------------- ------

T134 Spanner      Adjustable        11.99
T232 Wrench       Adjustable        13.55
```

The WHERE, or "row selection" conditions can be combined with "AND"s and "OR"s to compose queries which are as complex as you care to ask. If you wanted to know what products were adjustable or electrical (a little wacky but just suppose...), the command would be:

SELECT * FROM PRODUCTS WHERE
DESCRIPTION = ' Adjustable ' OR
DESCRIPTION = ' Electrical ';

giving:

```
CODE ITEM         DESCRIPTION        PRICE
---- ------------ ---------------- -----

T134 Spanner      Adjustable        11.99
T232 Wrench       Adjustable        13.55
T179 Pliers       Electrical         9.95
```

If someone asks "Have you got any spanners for less than $10?" the command:

SELECT * FROM PRODUCTS WHERE ITEM = ' Spanner ' AND PRICE < 10;

will do the job:

```
CODE ITEM          DESCRIPTION        PRICE
---- ------------  ----------------   -----
T135 Spanner       9/16 inch           7.25
T114 Spanner       7/16 inch           4.89
```

You don't have to enter the whole of a character field. If you just specify:

... WHERE ITEM LIKE ' Sp% '

you will retrieve all items with Sp as the first two letters. The character % in a LIKE clause means "any number (including zero) of any characters."

The % can be put in any position; if you specify:

... WHERE ITEM LIKE ' %s '

You will retrieve all items ending in "s," in this case "Pliers." If you specify:

... WHERE ITEM LIKE ' %er% '

you are asking for "all items with the letters "er" in any position including the beginning or the end." So you will get "Spanner" displayed as well as "Pliers."

This type of operation, where only certain rows are selected from a table, is known as "selection." While, logically enough, selection is done with a SELECT command in SQL, you will note that the projection operations are also done with SELECT.

The WHERE clause is sometimes referred to as the "predicate."

7.4 Sorting rows in order

Very often in business, one needs to see data arranged in a certain order: zipcode order, alphabetical order or last name, by size of transaction, and so on. To see the products arranged in order of increasing price, the command is simply:

SELECT * FROM PRODUCTS ORDER BY PRICE;

producing the listing:

```
CODE ITEM           DESCRIPTION       PRICE
---- ------------   ----------------  -----

T114 Spanner        7/16 inch          4.89
T135 Spanner        9/16 inch          7.25
T177 Pliers         Long nose          8.19
T179 Pliers         Electrical         9.95
T134 Spanner        Adjustable        11.99
T232 Wrench         Adjustable        13.55
```

SQL will present the result in ascending order unless told otherwise; to see the products sorted in descending price order, just add DESCENDING, or DESC:

SELECT * FROM PRODUCTS ORDER BY PRICE DESC;

which duly gives:

```
CODE ITEM           DESCRIPTION       PRICE
---- ------------   ----------------  -----

T232 Wrench         Adjustable        13.55
T134 Spanner        Adjustable        11.99
T179 Pliers         Electrical         9.95
T177 Pliers         Long nose          8.19
T114 Spanner        7/16 inch          4.89
T135 Spanner        9/16 inch          7.25
```

Of course, column selection, row selection and ordering can all be combined in the same SELECT statement if you want, as in:

```
SELECT CODE, PRICE FROM PRODUCTS
        WHERE ITEM = ' Spanner ' OR PRICE > 10
            ORDER BY PRICE DESC;                    giving:
```

```
CODE  PRICE
----  -----

T232  13.55
T134  11.99
T135   7.25
T114   4.89
```

Also, the ORDER BY column does not have to be numeric; if you use   . . . ORDER BY ITEM, the result will be sorted into alphabetical order on ITEM. And when you list the columns you want to see, they appear in the order in which you list them, not in their order in the base table. So:

```
    SELECT ITEM, CODE FROM PRODUCTS
        WHERE PRICE > 9
            ORDER BY PRICE;                    will give:
```

```
ITEM            CODE
------------    ----

Pliers          T179
Spanner         T134
Wrench          T232
```

Compare the codes with the original table and note that the products are in order of PRICE.

You can sort on several, or all, columns. For instance,

```
    SELECT * FROM PRODUCTS
        ORDER BY ITEM DESC, PRICE DESC;
```

first arranges the items in reverse alphabetical order, then within each item that has the same name, lists the most costly first, giving:

```
CODE ITEM          DESCRIPTION      PRICE
---- ------------  ---------------- -----

T232 Wrench        Adjustable       13.55
T134 Spanner       Adjustable       11.99
T135 Spanner       9/16 inch         7.25
T114 Spanner       7/16 inch         4.89
T179 Pliers        Electrical        9.95
T177 Pliers        Long nose         8.19
```

Syntax of the SELECT statement

We can summarize the possibilities that we have seen for a SELECT statement as shown below, using the normal conventions for syntax (statement form) by which:

| means   OR,

[   ]   means that whatever is inside the square brackets is optional.

BOLDFACE CAPITALS means a key word that must be in the statement.

A word in italics means a *variable* that is to be filled in as appropriate.

SELECT * | *column-name* [*,column-name* ...] FROM *table-name*

> *Select all columns OR a list of one or more columns*
> *from table-name.*

[WHERE *column-name* CO *value* [AND|OR *column-name* CO *value* ...]

> *Optionally, select rows where the value in a column has*
> *a certain relation to a value you supply. CO means*
> *"comparison operator" such as = > or <.*

[ORDER BY *column-name* [DESC]]

> *Optionally, sort rows into order by a given column*
> *name; in ascending order unless descending is specified.*

More complex forms of SELECT are possible; SQL allows very complex questions to be asked of databases of all sizes, as we shall see shortly.

126

7.5   Changing stored values

Once a row exists in a table, the values in it can be changed with an UPDATE command. For example:

UPDATE PRODUCTS SET PRICE = 15.95 WHERE CODE = ' T232 ' ;

will change the price of adjustable wrenches from their existing value to $15.95.

The "WHERE" condition can be any specification which identifies the row you want to change, for example:

. . . . WHERE ITEM = ' Wrench ' AND DESCRIPTION = ' Adjustable '

If there is no ...WHERE clause, *all* the rows will be updated, which could be very undesirable. If you have 10,000 products, and accidentally set the price of every one to $15.95, it could be an expensive mistake.

Partly for this reason, most relational DBMS's provide a ROLLBACK command. If you should enter an incorrect command (like the disastrous UPDATE), you can enter "ROLLBACK" and the database will be restored to the position before you issued the UPDATE.

In fact, ROLLBACK restores the database to the position after you entered the last COMMIT command.   After changing the database, you have an opportunity to consider whether what you have done is correct, before entering COMMIT.   So you could issue two UPDATE statements, and then look at the changed row(s) with a SELECT statement to see that the UPDATE(s) have had the effect you want.   The database is not permanently changed until you enter "COMMIT."

You should also remember that if there should be a hardware problem, or a software interrupt, the DBMS will automatically roll back the database to the position that it was in when you last COMMITted. This can be very annoying if you have done a number of complex changes without entering COMMIT; all your work is lost. It is good practice, therefore, to issue a COMMIT each time you are sure that the database is in a consistent state.

You can change more than one value with a simple UPDATE statement.   The general syntax is:

UPDATE *table-name* SET *column-name* = *value* [, *column-name* = *value* , ...]

> WHERE *condition*;

Removing data

DELETE FROM *table-name* WHERE *condition*

> removes all the rows that meet the WHERE condition

DELETE FROM *table-name*

> removes all rows but leaves the table still useable

DROP TABLE *table-name*

> removes the whole table from the data dictionary; if you want to use it again, you will have to enter a fresh CREATE TABLE statement.

7.6   Adding columns to a table

If it becomes necessary to add columns to a table after it has been created, an ALTER TABLE statement can be issued. For example:

ALTER TABLE PRODUCTS ADD IN_STOCK_QTY NUMBER(4);

would add a column to the PRODUCTS table.

None of the existing data in the table is affected: all the SELECT statements which use the table will still give exactly the same results, except for SELECT * FROM PRODUCTS, which will now display five columns, instead of four. (For this reason, SELECT * FROM PRODUCTS should only be used for one-time only queries; all application programs which will be used again and again should have SELECT statements which explicitly list the columns to be retrieved.)

Some relational DBMSs (such as ORACLE) allow an existing column in a table to be widened, for example with:

ALTER TABLE PRODUCTS MODIFY IN_STOCK_QTY NUMBER(5);

Clearly, the ALTER statement gives great flexibility to a system, and makes it responsive to changing business needs.

7.7   Sub-queries

Suppose you wanted to know which products cost more than the electrical pliers. You could get the answer in two steps. First enter:

SELECT PRICE FROM PRODUCTS WHERE CODE = ' T179 '

which would give
```
PRICE
-----
9.95
```

then enter:

SELECT * FROM PRODUCTS WHERE PRICE > 9.95

However, SQL has a powerful "sub-query" facility which allows you to get the answer in one step by combining the two SELECT statements:

SELECT * FROM PRODUCTS WHERE PRICE >
             (SELECT PRICE FROM PRODUCTS WHERE CODE = ' T179 ')

SQL processes the SELECT statement in parentheses first, and then uses the value so obtained to process the first SELECT statement.

Whenever you have a question which is posed in terms of an attribute of a named entity (for example, the price of the pliers), rather than the value of the attribute itself ($9.95), a sub-query is implied.

"What costs more than the pliers?"

"What product has a price greater than the price of the pliers?"

"Who earns less than Jones?"

"What employees have a salary less than Jones' salary?"

"What firms have a higher ROI than IBM?

"What firms have an ROI greater than IBM's ROI?"

A sub-query may be used to derive the most recent record from a history table. Suppose you have a table of employees, which does not hold their current salaries.   Each time a person's salary is changed, a row is inserted in the SALARY_HISTORY table, giving the new salary, and the date it becomes effective.

Then, each time a query is made which involves a person's current salary (or during payroll processing), the SALARY_HISTORY table has to be scanned to find the latest (maximum) effective date for a given employee, and thus their current salary.

```
EMPLOYEES

PERSON_ID FN          LN
--------- ----------  ----------
    26633 Robert      Brown
    70904 Fred        Smith
       .
       .
       .



SALARY_HISTORY

PERSON_ID EFFECTIVE SALARY
--------- --------- ------
    26633 01-APR-85  22000
    70904 15-MAY-85  24500
       .
    26633 30-JUN-86  25000
       .
```

Inspection of the tables shows that Robert Brown (26633) was most recently given a raise on 30 June 1986, to $25,000. The query to retrieve this from the database is:

SELECT SALARY FROM SALARY_HISTORY

WHERE PERSON_ID =
  (SELECT PERSON_ID FROM EMPLOYEES WHERE FN = ' Robert ' AND LN = ' Brown ')

  AND EFFECTIVE =
  (SELECT MAX(EFFECTIVE) FROM SALARY_HISTORY
    WHERE PERSON_ID =
  (SELECT PERSON_ID FROM EMPLOYEES WHERE FN = ' Robert' AND LN = ' Brown '))

7.8 Joining tables

Suppose you have two tables describing sales: SALES and SALE_ITEMS.

SELECT * FROM SALES   gives:

```
SALE_NO SPN SALE_DATE
------- --- ---------
   1001 AAA 10-SEP-86
   1002 BBB 10-SEP-86
```
(SPN is the salesperson's initials)

SELECT * FROM SALE_ITEMS   gives:

```
SALE_NO LINE_NO CODE    QTY
------- ------- ----  -----
   1001       1 H995      2
   1001       2 H134      5
   1001       3 T232      3
   1002       1 T134      1
   1002       2 P121      4
```

By comparing the two tables, you can see that sale 1001 consisted of the purchase of 3 products: two H995s, five H134's and three T232's. Likewise, sale 1002 consisted of the purchase of one T134 and four P121's. If we wanted to produce a single listing combining the two tables, our first thought might be:

SELECT * FROM SALES , SALE_ITEMS

which would give the interesting listing:

```
SALE_NO SPN SALE_DATE   SALE_NO LINE_NO CODE    QTY
------- --- ---------   ------- ------- ----  ------
   1001 AAA 10-SEP-86       1001       1 H995     2
   1002 BBB 10-SEP-86       1001       1 H995     2
   1001 AAA 10-SEP-86       1001       2 H134     5
   1002 BBB 10-SEP-86       1001       2 H134     5
   1001 AAA 10-SEP-86       1001       3 T232     3
   1002 BBB 10-SEP-86       1001       3 T232     3
   1001 AAA 10-SEP-86       1002       1 T134     1
   1002 BBB 10-SEP-86       1002       1 T134     1
   1001 AAA 10-SEP-86       1002       2 P121     4
   1002 BBB 10-SEP-86       1002       2 P121     4
```

This combines both tables all right, but it doesn't mean much. As you can see, what SQL has done is to take the entire SALES table, and add the first row of SALE_ITEMS to each of its two rows. Then it has taken the SALES table again, and added to it the second row of SALE_ITEMS, and so on, making a combined table which covers all the possible combinations of rows. You'll note it has 10 rows (5 rows in SALE_ITEMS times 2 rows in SALES); such an exhaustive combined table is known in the jargon as the "Cartesian product" of the two tables.

SALE_NO appears twice; it is the column that both tables have in common. This fact brings us to the realization that we are only interested in combinations where the SALE_NO in SALES is the same as the SALE_NO in SALE_ITEMS; a row like the second row above combining the details of number 1002 with an item from 1001 really has no meaning. It follows that we must select only those rows that make sense, with:

```
SELECT * FROM SALES , SALE_ITEMS
        WHERE SALES . SALE_NO = SALE_ITEMS . SALE_NO
```

(Note that to specify which SALE_NO is meant, the column-name is prefixed with its table-name followed by a period.) The result is:

```
SALE_NO SPN SALE_DATE SALE_NO LINE_NO CODE    QTY
------- --- --------- ------- ------- ----  ------
   1001 AAA 10-SEP-86    1001       1 H995       2
   1001 AAA 10-SEP-86    1001       2 H134       5
   1001 AAA 10-SEP-86    1001       3 T232       3
   1002 BBB 10-SEP-86    1002       1 T134       1
   1002 BBB 10-SEP-86    1002       2 P121       4
```

Now we have only 5 rows, corresponding to the 5 items in our 2 SALES, and each row is relevant to one single item.

To prevent SALE_NO from appearing twice, we have to list out the columns in the order in which we want them to appear, for example:

```
SELECT SALES . SALE_NO, SPN, CODE, QTY, SALE_DATE
        FROM SALES, SALE_ITEMS
        WHERE SALES . SALE_NO = SALE_ITEMS . SALE_NO
```

In the list of column-names, SALE_ITEMS.SALE_NO could have been used instead of SALES.SALE_NO, and would have given the same result. However, you must avoid ambiguity by qualifying SALE_NO with one of the table-names, or you'll get the error message, "Column ambiguously defined."

Since any one sale involves updating tables, we have to reckon with the possibility that one of the updates might fail, so that we might end up with a SALE that has no SALE_ITEMS (a childless parent) or a SALE_ITEM that has no corresponding SALE (an orphan).

If this should happen, the database is said to have lost "referential integrity." Of course, it would be ideal if the DBMS would stop this happening. We would like to be able to say, when we create SALES and SALE_ITEMS, that there should never be a value of SALE_NO in one of the tables without at least one corresponding value in the other. But very few relational DBMS's support referential integrity at the time of writing.

You are not limited to joining only two tables; the report above would be more meaningful if it included ITEM and DESCRIPTION for each product sold, not just the CODE. ITEM and DESCRIPTION of course, will have to be extracted from the row in PRODUCTS corresponding to the CODE of the sale. So you could request:

```
SELECT          SALES . SALE_NO,
                SPN,
                CODE,
                ITEM,
                DESCRIPTION,
                QTY,
                SALE_DATE
                FROM PRODUCTS, SALE_ITEMS, SALES
                    WHERE SALES . SALE_NO = SALE_ITEMS . SALE_NO
                    AND PRODUCTS . CODE = SALE_ITEMS . CODE
```

which will give:

```
SALE_NO SPN CODE ITEM          DESCRIPTION        QTY SALE_DATE
------- --- ---- ------------- ----------------- --- ---------
   1001 AAA H995 Bucket        24 quart            2 10-SEP-86
   1001 AAA H134 Refuse bin    Pedal opening       5 10-SEP-86
   1001 AAA T232 Wrench        Adjustable          3 10-SEP-86
   1002 BBB T134 Spanner       Adjustable          1 10-SEP-86
   1002 BBB P121 Paintbrush    3 inch              4 10-SEP-86
```

You have thus made one table out of three.
(Note that we have added some more products to the original table.)

As you can see, in SQL there is no explicit JOIN command. Projection, selection, and joining of tables are all done with SELECT statements (which is why SQL is sometimes accused of being a "one-statement language").

7.9 Views

SQL allows the creation of apparent (or virtual) tables, which look and act like tables, but do not physically exist. For instance, this statement:

```
CREATE VIEW SALESTODAY                                          The columns
        ( SPN, CODE, ITEM, DESCRIPTION, PRICE, QTY, ITEM_TOTAL )  − of the view
   AS
SELECT SPN,                                              }
        CODE,                                            } This is
        ITEM,                                            } where the
        DESCRIPTION,                                     } data will
        PRICE,                                           } come from
        QTY,                                             }
        (PRICE * QTY )                                   }
FROM  PRODUCTS, SALES, SALE_ITEMS
WHERE  SALE_ITEMS . CODE = PRODUCTS . CODE
   AND  SALE_ITEMS . SALE_NO = SALES . SALE_NO
```

will cause a view named SALESTODAY to be defined in the data dictionary. There will be no actual physical SALESTODAY table: the data will still be held in the "base" tables (PRODUCTS, SALES, SALE_ITEMS).

However, if you now request:

```
SELECT * FROM SALESTODAY
```

you will get:

```
SPN CODE ITEM          DESCRIPTION        PRICE QTY ITEM_TOTAL
--- ---- ------------  -----------------  ------ --- ----------
AAA H995 Bucket        24 quart           10.95  1      10.95
AAA H134 Refuse bin    Pedal opening      13.25  2      26.50
 .
 .
 .
```

just as though this table existed. If any of the data in the base tables is changed, the view will be automatically changed as well. Once the view is created, it will stay defined until a DROP VIEW statement is issued (or one of the tables used in the CREATE VIEW statement is dropped).

SALESTODAY is a view which is made from a join: views can be defined on only one table. This is often done for security: one could define a view on a table which includes only the non-sensitive columns, and then allow people to access the view, but not to access the table.

7.10 Indexes

The tables which make up a relational database are usually stored on a moving-head disk drive. As you use larger and larger tables, speed of retrieval becomes more of an issue.

Suppose you want to know how many electrical pliers have been sold; say that SALE_ITEMS contains 10,000 rows. When you issue a command like:

SELECT * FROM SALE_ITEMS WHERE CODE = ' T179 '

the DBMS will carry out a "full table scan," that is, it will read the first row of the table, decide if the code is T179, display it if it is, or go on and read the next row if it is not, until it finds the required row, which means that it may have to read every row in the table.

This can take an appreciable time, unless the computer is so large that the whole table can be paged into main memory, and scanned there.

Now suppose that if, as well as the data table, one had also a side table, containing the numbers of the rows for each code value, like this:

```
Code            Row numbers

T177    17, 29, 93, 176, 211, 439, 512, 717, 893, 911
T179    3, 26, 114, 826, 993
T184    etc...
```

This side table is comparable to the index of a book, which shows the pages on which a word or topic appears. Given a code number, one could look in the side table, and then retrieve the rows required directly, which is much faster than reading every row.

(In fact an index created by SQL is a file which contains the addresses on disk where the relevant rows are stored.)

If, after creating a table such as SALE_ITEMS, you want to create an index to the values of CODE, you enter:

CREATE INDEX CODE_NDX ON SALE_ITEMS (CODE)

SQL will create a side table for the index; every time SALE_ITEMS is changed, the index will be automatically updated. (CODE_NDX is a name which you choose for the index.)

Each relational DBMS contains an optimizer software facility, which analyzes each SQL command and decides how it can best be carried out.

If you enter:

SELECT * FROM SALE_ITEMS WHERE CODE = ' T179 ' ;

the optimizer will look at the column used in the WHERE clause (CODE in this case). If an index exists, and if using the index will speed up response to the query, the optimizer will use it. If an index does not exist, the optimizer will use a full table scan to handle the query. The significant thing is that you write the SELECT statement in just the same way whether or not an index exists.

An index can be created on a combination of columns. Thus if the key to SALE_ITEMS is the concatenation of SALE_NO and LINE_NO, you could create an index to that key with

CREATE INDEX ITEM_NDX ON SALE_ITEMS (SALE_NO, LINE_NO)

Of course, as we discussed earlier, you want the key to be unique. You can enforce this through the index with:

CREATE UNIQUE INDEX ITEM_NDX ON SALE_ITEMS (SALE_NO, LINE_NO)

Once a unique index has been created, if anyone attempts to insert a row with a combination of SALE_NO and LINE_NO which already exists, it will be rejected.

The general syntax of the CREATE INDEX statement is:

CREATE [UNIQUE] INDEX *index-name* ON *table-name* (*column-name* [, *column-name* ...])

In the next chapter, we will discuss the issue of what indexes should be created for any given table.

More information about table processing operations can be found in "A guide to DB2" by Chris Date (Addison-Wesley, 1984).

Exercises and discussion points.

1. Using the table on page 7-1, write a SELECT statement to show the CODE and PRICE for all spanners, listed in descending order of PRICE.

2. Write the CREATE TABLE statements to set up the SALES and SALE_ITEMS tables on page 7-13.

3. Write a SELECT statement which will join SALES and SALE_ITEMS and produce a listing showing only SALE_DATE, SALE_NO, CODE, and QTY.

4. Assuming SALES and SALE_ITEMS are large tables, what indexes do you think should be created for them?

5. If you have access to a system which can run SQL, create SALES and SALE_ITEMS, and insert 1000 records into SALES, with 5 items per sale. Time how long it takes to respond to a query which joins the two tables, first without indexes, then with SALE_NO indexed in both tables.

Chapter 8

Improving performance of a relational database system

8.1   Why performance is an issue

With non-relational DBMS's (such as IMS), it is usual to store as much information as possible in a single physical record.   To take a simplified example, all the data describing all the items in a given sale might be stored in one physical record, so that it could all be located with one movement of the disk read-head.

With a relational DBMS, the data is often divided up amongst two or more tables, as we have seen, usually stored at different locations on the disk. Consequently, each time a query is made which involves the joining of two more tables, the disk head must move repeatedly from table to table to locate the rows needed to answer the query.   Even though the average time to move the disk head from one track to another is of the order of 10 milliseconds, it only takes 1000 such movements to produce a response time of 10 seconds or more, which is often unacceptable.

Note that this problem only arises when the data is stored on disk; if main memory is large enough to allow the relevant parts of the table(s) to be paged in, the joining of the tables takes place at CPU speed, and performance is much less of an issue.   As operating systems (such as MVS/ESA) are introduced which can support larger address spaces, and main memory becomes cheaper and cheaper, relational DBMS vendors will increasingly seek to improve performance by trying to ensure that all the data needed to handle a query is paged in by the time it is needed.

8.2   Speeding up retrieval with indexes

As we discussed in the previous chapter, creation of an index speeds up retrieval of data from a table by specifying where on disk the relevant row(s) are to be found.   Thus, in principle, any given row can be found by two movements of the disk head (one to the index, plus one to the given location in the table), rather than by however many movements are needed to search the whole table.

This additional speed of retrieval costs two things: disk space for the index, and additional time for each update because the index has to be updated as well as the base table. If plenty of disk space is available, the additional space needed for indexes may not be a problem. Similarly, in many applications it is not crucial whether it takes 1 second or 3 seconds to update a table. But the more indexes that are created, the slower the updates will be and the more disk space will be taken up. Generally speaking therefore, one should create the minimum number of indexes to give adequate performance, as follows:

1.   The key identifier of each table should have a unique index created for it. This has to be done anyway to ensure uniqueness of the key value, but is also important for performance since

   a)   the key is likely to be the most frequent search argument used for update and retrieval

   b)   the key is likely to be the column used to join the table to other tables.

2.   Next the foreign keys in each table should be indexed.   (Foreign keys are columns or concatenations of columns which hold values that are the values of keys in other tables, sometimes referred to as "other-relation keys.")

   Looking at the structure of the three tables we used in the previous chapter:

SALES		SALE_ITEMS		PRODUCTS	
K	SALE_NO	K	SALE_NO	K	CODE
	SPN	K	LINE_NO		ITEM
	SALE_DATE		CODE		DESCRIPTION
			QTY		PRICE

we see that, assuming that the key columns are already indexed, the only foreign key needing to be indexed is the product code in SALE_ITEMS, namely SALE_ITEMS.CODE. This will speed up retrievals from SALE_ITEMS such as "How many T179's have been sold?" and will speed up any join of SALE_ITEMS and PRODUCTS.

Obviously foreign keys should be indexed non-uniquely; T179 will be the CODE in many SALE_ITEMS.

3. Next, each column which may be used in a rapid-response query should be considered as a candidate for indexing. For instance, SALE_DATE above, though not a foreign key, might be worth indexing in order to speed up queries like "How many sales have been made today so far?". In tables which describe people, LAST_NAME is often worth indexing because it is frequently used to access records, even though it is not a key or a foreign key. In considering candidates for indexing, you should include queries which will be made through screen applications: they will also generate SELECT .... FROM .... WHERE .... statements that will use indexes provided they are available.

4. Columns which are used for sorting, in ORDER BY .... clauses, are candidates for being indexed. In some cases, the sorting goes faster if the column(s) being used has been declared as NOT NULL when the table was created.

8.3 Speeding up retrieval by "realizing" joins

If, no matter what indexes are created, the response time or throughput for a SELECT statement involving a join is not acceptable, you should consider the more serious step of "realizing" the join, that is to say, physically combining two or more tables to make a joined table, which is maintained as one table.

The first such type of join to consider is the one involved with code interpretation, discussed in Section 6.5. If the data is stored in 4NF, as shown in the example

```
1.   FLT_NO    DEPARTS    FROM_CODE    TO_CODE
     ------    -------    ---------    -------

     996       1230       SFO          JFK
      .
      .
      .


2.   CODE    AIRPORT_NAME
     ----    ----------------

     DFW     Dallas-Fort Worth
     JFK     New York-Kennedy
     SFO     San Francisco
      .
      .
```

then every time a ticket is written, the two tables will have to be joined (twice, in fact, since both origin and destination are involved). If, in spite of indexing the three code columns, the response time is still not adequate, the 4NF design may be compromised ("denormalized"), back to the original 2NF table:

```
FLT_NO DEPARTS FROM_AIRPORT       CODE TO_AIRPORT        CODE
------ ------- ----------------   ---- ----------------  ----

996    1230    San Francisco      SFO  New York-Kennedy  JFK
 .
 .
 .
```

Clearly, this will involve a lot of redundancy: assuming there are 500 flights leaving JFK and 500 arriving, then storing "New York-Kennedy" in the realized join will need 18,000 characters more (for that one airport) than storing it once in the STATION_CODES table. But the response time improvement can be dramatic.

Another case of realizing joins arises when two tables are in a one-to-many relationship, like SALES and SALE_ITEMS. If the joining involved in displaying all details of a given sale takes too long in spite of SALE_NO being indexed in both tables, then you may consider storing the physically joined table, perhaps called SALES_DETAILS:

```
SALE_NO  LINE_NO  SPN  SALE_DATE   CODE   QTY
-------  -------  ---  ---------   ----   -----

   1001        1  AAA  10-SEP-86   H995       2
   1001        2  AAA  10-SEP-86   H134       5
   1001        3  AAA  10-SEP-86   T232       3
   1002        1  BBB  10-SEP-86   T134       1
   1002        2  BBB  10-SEP-86   P121       4
```

Here there is considerable duplication (of SPN and SALE_DATE); the table is not even in 2NF, but in 1NF. However, the response time to a query such as "How many T179's did we sell yesterday?" which would imply a join on the original 2 tables, will be much better.

As an aside, the issue of referential integrity should of course not arise with the realized join: a small added benefit.

8.4 Speeding up retrieval by storing summary data

Even if you have joined SALES and SALE_ITEMS into one SALES_DETAILS table, you may still find that it takes too long to answer queries that involve summarization. Assume that SALES_DETAILS contains all the sales for the last 90 days (say 90,000 rows), and you want to know the sales of T179's for the last 7 days, last 14 days, last 21 days and last 28 days, to see a crude trend. You would need to say:

```
SELECT SUM(QTY) FROM SALES_DETAILS
     WHERE CODE = ' T179 '
          AND (TODAYS_DATE - SALE_DATE) < 7
```

and then repeat the statement for 14 days, and so on. (Some versions of SQL enable the summaries to be done in one statement.) Even if CODE and SALE_DATE are indexed, as we suggested, this query will probably still take too long for an acceptable on-line response; it will almost certainly take too long if the join has not been realized.

A solution here is to have a special summary table, perhaps with the structure:

```
SALES_SUMMARIES
     CODE
     SALES_LAST_7_DAYS
     SALES_LAST_14_DAYS
     SALES_LAST_21_DAYS
     SALES_LAST_28_DAYS
```

Every night, or every weekend, a batch routine containing the series of SELECT statements is run, and the sales summaries are updated. Then, given a value of CODE, the response to a query is immediate. The drawback to this, as of all off-line summarization, is that the data may be stale (for example, if you inquire on a Thursday about the last 7 days, and the update routine was last run at the weekend). Worse, its staleness may not be apparent to the casual user (unless the table includes information about when it was last updated).

The "current value" problem, such as determining someone's current salary, or a customer's current balance, poses similar problems. If it takes too long to compute current salary from SALARY_HISTORY table (as we discussed in Section 7.7), then the value of current salary can be stored in the EMPLOYEES table, and updated every time a new row is inserted in SALARY_HISTORY. To guard against the possibility of this update failing (and CURRENT_SALARY being stale), a nightly integrity-checking routine could include a module which compares the value of everyone's CURRENT_SALARY with their most recent record in SALARY_HISTORY, and prints out a message if a discrepancy is found.

Exercises and discussion points:

1. Considering the system discussed in Chapter 1, which columns in which tables do you think should be indexed uniquely? Which should be indexed, but non-uniquely?

2. Why should the issue of referential integrity not arise with a realized join?

3. If you have access to a system which can run SQL, take the SALES and SALE_ITEMS tables you created in Exercise 5 of the previous chapter, and create a realized join of the two tables. Compare the disk space used by the two original tables with that used by the realized join.

4. In what sort of business application do you think the problem of stale data is critical? Can you suggest some ways of minimizing the risk that managers will make faulty decisions because they are using stale information?

Chapter 9

Transforming the logical model into a physical model

In Chapters 4, 5 and 6, we considered techniques for defining and specifying the underlying logical essence of an information system. The logical model, consisting of a system-wide DFD with a description of each process, an entity-relationship model, and a group of normalized tables describing the contents of each datastore, describes *what* the system data and processing will be.

In Chapter 8, we considered *how* the data would need to be physically stored to meet the objectives of the system, in terms of response time to queries, and run-time for batch processes. In this chapter, we consider how the logical processes on the DFD should be assigned to physical procedures.

9.1   Pre-implementation data model compromises

As hardware becomes faster, there is more and more of a case for implementing the system at first with the 4NF relations as actual physical tables. This produces a physical database which is simple, non-redundant, and easy to change. If, once the system is running, response times are not acceptable, joins can be realized judiciously, and summary data stored where necessary.

However, so long as moving head disks are used for storage, it is always worth reviewing the probable performance of the "pure" 4NF database in the light of table sizes and system objectives, and possibly compromising the pure design in sensible ways even before the system is implemented. For instance, code-interpretation tables can be merged back into the tables containing the codes; summary data tables can be defined to avoid processing large tables on-line.

Compromises like this should be made by, or in consultation with, an experienced database administrator (DBA). Indeed, the application designer is well-advised to consult with the DBA before drafting the entity-relationship diagram (in case there are parts of the corporate data model which can be adopted, to save time and improve overall integrity), and to review the logical data model with the DBA once it is completed.

9.2 Partitioning the system-wide DFD into procedure-units

As we noted in Chapter 1, the system-wide DFD needs to be divided into chunks of automated and/or manual procedures which can be executed (and therefore developed) as units.

In this book, the term "procedure-unit" (PU) is used for these chunks: a procedure-unit may be a program, or a manual procedure, or a stored command list, or some combination of the three. A procedure-unit is always invoked as a unit (whether from a menu or by operator commands), and is seen by the users of the system as a unit. Its name can be substituted for X in the sentences:

> "Now we're going to run X"
> "We've finished the X; what do we do next?"

Thus the following could be procedure-units:

Sales order entry procedure	(Manual procedure plus program)
Bank deposit preparation	(Manual procedure)
Fund performance analysis program	(Program which captures latest prices plus program which values portfolios plus program which ranks funds and generates report)

The following would probably not be procedure-units:

Management reporting	(probably multiple procedure-units run at different times)
Internal rate-of-return calculation	(probably a component of a project evaluation procedure-unit)

To partition the DFD:

1.   Consider each input.   When or under what circumstances will it arrive? Input transactions may arrive continuously, as with a retail store or a telephone sales operation, or in batches, as with incoming mail or tapes/disks received from other systems.

What is the largest area of the DFD that can be seen as being activated to handle the given input?   (Choosing the largest area gives you the best chance to have a system with the fewest possible work tables, and therefore the best inherent performance.)

Is there any reason why this largest area of the DFD should not be implemented as a single procedure-unit?   It may be that the size of the code required would exceed the available main memory (less likely as memories get larger).   It may be that a single candidate procedure-unit needs to be split because, for reasons of control or security, it is desirable to have different functions performed by different groups.   Consider the fragment of a system-wide DFD shown here:

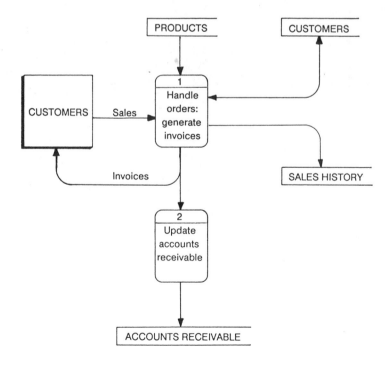

Other things being equal, the whole of this fragment could technically be implemented as one procedure-unit. The salesperson would take the order and enter it into the system, which would create a new customer record if necessary, generate the invoice and insert the invoice details into the ACCOUNTS_RECEIVABLE data store. However, since this represents the books of the business, it might be desirable, for control reasons, to have Process #1 simply write the sale data into the SALES_HISTORY data store, and then have a separate procedure-unit, controlled by the Accounts Department, which would generate the invoice and update ACCOUNTS_RECEIVABLE. If this alternative is chosen, the "physicalized" DFD would look slightly different:

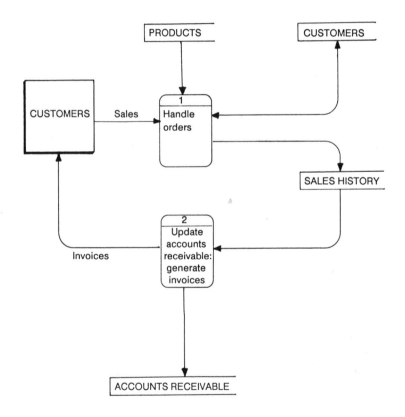

2.   Next, consider each output. When or under what circumstances is it to be produced? Is it similar in data structure and timing to any other outputs? If

so, could the processes generating the two outputs be combined? As with each input, ask yourself: What is the largest area of the DFD that can be seen as being active at one time to generate the output(s)? Is there any reason why this area of the DFD should not be implemented as a single procedure-unit? For example, in Chapter 1, we saw that a single system-wide process ("Determine re-order quantity and supplier"), in fact, needed to be implemented as three procedure-units.

3.   Once the procedure-units associated with each input and each output have been defined, and their boundaries marked on the DFD, there may be some parts of the logical model which have not yet been included in the procedure-units already defined. They should now be partitioned into procedure-units. Once again, the aim should be to define the fewest procedure-units that will meet the system's objectives.

Once all the processes on the system-wide logical DFD have been assigned to procedure-units, the "housekeeping" procedure-units should be considered. These include:

- procedure-units to carry out routine maintenance of object data stores, for example, to insert new customers, handle changes to customer records, and delete inactive customers. At least one procedure-unit will be needed for each data store on the DFD that was marked with "RM."

- procedure-units to purge old event records from the active database to some archival storage. Once a sale has been delivered to the customer and paid for, the details may be kept in the active database for 90 or 180 days, or even longer, depending on the business requirements. At some point, however, each sale or purchase or payment or delivery record will no longer be worth keeping in the database, and will need to be archived. This may be done by copying the row to an old-history table, and deleting the row from the active-history table.

   The old-history table may then be kept in the database (where it will take up disk space) or exported to disk or tape (from which it could be restored to the database if it were ever needed).

- procedure-units to back up the database (if this is not provided as a system utility).

- an "integrity-checker" procedure-unit. As we noted in Chapter 7, the fact that data about a single entity, like a sale, may be stored in two tables means that errors can arise where a record can be in one table without a corresponding record in the other. Whenever you suspect that such referential integrity might be lost, you should add a statement to the integrity-checker routine, which will typically be run every night.

For example, to detect any orphan SALES_ITEMS, you might write:

SELECT * FROM SALES_ITEMS WHERE SALE_NO NOT IN
(SELECT SALE_NO FROM SALES)

If the database has referential integrity, this will result in a message such as "No records retrieved" but if a sale item record is printed out, you clearly have a problem which must be investigated with some urgency.

When all the procedure-units have been defined, a master list can be drawn up, similar to the one included in Chapter 1.

The issue arises as to whether the original identifiers of processes on the logical DFD should be preserved,   or whether each procedure-unit should be represented by one process on a "physicalized" DFD.

If the original identifiers are to be preserved, the procedure-units should be given numbers which correspond to the logical processes implemented.   If a procedure-unit implements, say processes 2 and 4 and 9, it should be identified as 2+4+9.   If a given process, say #13, is subdivided into several procedure-units, they should have numbers 13-1, 13-2, and so on.

The decision as to whether to preserve the "logical" numbering, or to renumber procedure-units on a "physicalized" DFD turns on whether it is likely that you will ever want to return to the purely logical model to consider other physical options.   If so, there is an argument for preserving and maintaining the logical model.   On the other hand, (particularly since with 4GLs there may not be many discrepancies between logical and physical), if it is likely that the physical system will not be re-automated for some years, it is probably simpler to go ahead and renumber each process box, making each correspond to one procedure-unit.

Exercises and discussion points:

1.   Consider a system which has been implemented, and for which you have the data flow diagram.   Divide it into procedure-units using the approach given in this chapter.   What differences are there, if any, between these procedure-units and the actual programs which implement the system?   Can you account for these differences?

2.   What are the archiving procedures for event records in some systems that you are familiar with?

Chapter 10

Specifying the logic of procedure units

Once the master list of procedure units has been drawn up, with each related to the data flow diagram, and so to the tables of the database, their development and testing must be planned. Normally, a written specification for a procedure unit is produced and reviewed; this specification in theory contains all the information necessary for someone who knows the target language to produce the code for the procedure unit.

Depending on the language which will be used to implement the procedure unit, and division of labor involved, the formality of the specification can vary. Indeed, as fourth-generation languages (4GLs) become more powerful, the code will get more and more to resemble a specification, so that eventually the specification will wither away as a separate document and each procedure unit will be generated directly by someone who knows the business. Some interesting developments along this line are described in the next chapter.

10.1   Division of labor

Three broad "degrees of division of labor" can be seen:

- "one-head" implementation, in which the business analyst is also responsible for coding and testing, probably using a powerful 4GL. It is likely that this will be common practice in the future.

- "two-head" implementation, in which the business analyst specifies the procedure unit, and one or more implementers code and test, *but working in close contact with the analyst*.

- "over-the-wall" implementation, in which the analyst(s) produces a detailed "quasi-legal document" as specification which is then transmitted ("thrown over the wall") to the coders, who have to code and test without much interaction with the analysts. This situation may occur when the coders are in another building (or another city), or when the coding is done under contract.

Clearly, the level of specification involved, and the effort and time involved in producing it, varies greatly with this degree of division of labor.

With a one-head implementation, the procedure unit need only be specified to the point where the implementer has a clear mental picture of the input and output formats, and of the internal logic. The area of the dataflow diagram involved has been defined, and the tables to be accessed have also been defined. If the screens are to be generated with a screen painter, the analyst/implementer should know what fields will appear on each screen, but can use the screen painter itself to work out their exact row and column location. Conversely, if the target language requires the screen format to be coded in detail, it will probably save time to produce an exact screen layout before starting to code.

With a two-head implementation, the analyst needs to hand over:

- the system-wide DFD
- data store and table contents with explanations of each data element
- the master list of procedure units
- any screen and report layouts that have been defined so far for the procedure unit under consideration
- notes for dialogue scripts and procedure logic for the procedure unit.

The implementers need to be briefed on the business background and the objectives of the system. The material developed by the analyst should be presented in a walk-through, in which the implementers can ask all the questions they need. If any procedure units are to be prototyped, it is probably most productive for the implementers to do so; they may also work with user representatives to refine details of formats and logic. The line between analysis and implementation is fuzzy in a two-head project; the implementers should be brought into the project as soon as enough analysis has been done for them to be productive. If group interview techniques are being used, as discussed in Chapter 3, this is often after the data/process sessions; the implementers will thus participate in relevant screens-and-reports sessions.

With over-the-wall implementation, the analyst needs to document each screen and report, and specify the business logic of each procedure unit, as well as documenting the database design,   and specifying the background to the project.   The techniques described in this chapter, such as action diagrams, may be used.

10.2   Dialogue formats

No matter what the degree of division of labor, it is important and tricky to think clearly about multi-screen dialogues.   There are often three actors in the dialogue: the operator, the system, and someone on the phone with whom the operator is having a conversation.   The dialogue may branch depending on what the caller says and what the system says, and the branching structure itself needs to be planned and controlled.   There are two approaches to specifying dialogues: the multi-column script and the playscript.

Multi-column script

The next page shows a sample multi-column display.

In column 1, the external events and conditions which trigger the dialogue are tabulated (including things the caller says), together with labels for the control flow and logical connectors, such as IF and ELSE.

In column 2, the operator's actions are tabulated, other than entering data into the system, which is in column 3.   Columns 4 and 5 tabulate the system's external and internal actions, respectively.

If there were no human dialogue, the chart might need only columns 3, 4 and 5, which would correspond to the system's input, output and processing respectively.   If one wants to concentrate only on the human dialogue and/or manual procedures, they are shown in columns 1 and 2.

The multi-column script lends itself to being built up piecemeal, perhaps in a group workshop.   Large pieces of paper are ruled with the five columns; each entry may be written on an adhesive label, so that it can easily be moved around as the dialogue evolves.

External event/ condition	Operator says/does	Operator enters	System displays	System action
START			Main menu	
Caller says something like "I'm interested in [author]'s book on [subject], [title]		I for Inquiry/Order		GO TO Screen 1
ELSE IF				
Caller says:				
"I ordered a book and it hasn't come" OR "You sent me wrong/ damaged book"		E for Existing order		GO TO Screen 2
ELSE IF				
Caller says anything else		P for Problems		GO TO Screen 3

Screen 1: Inquiry/order   Invoked from: Main menu

(The screen layout may be inserted here or kept in a separate part of the document)

External event/ condition	Operator says/does	Operator enters	System displays	System action
		Whatever info caller gave		Retrieve books based on author name, and/or subject, and/or title keywords
IF no hit, or too many to read out				
	Ask caller for more info			
ELSE	Give caller price and delivery, Ask for order			
IF caller does not want to order,				
	Thank for calling		Esc	GO TO START
ELSE	Ask for shipment details			
	. . .			

Play script

The other representation of a dialogue is the playscript, so called because it is similar to the text of a play, with the addition of a left-hand column to hold labels and logical connectors as shown here:

Label/ logic	Player	Action
START	System	Displays main menu
IF	Caller	Says something like "I'm interested in [author]'s book on [subject], [title]..."
THEN	Operator	Enters I for Inquiry/Order
	System	GO TO Screen 1
ELSE IF	Caller	Says "I ordered a book and it hasn't come" OR "You sent me wrong/damaged book"
THEN	Operator	Says "Sorry, let me get your record"
		Enters E for Existing Order
	System	GO TO Screen 2
ELSE IF	Caller	Says anything else
THEN	Operator	Enter P for Problems
	System	GO TO Screen 3.
.		
.		

This representation stresses the sequence of events, but does not make it so easy to separate the two conversations.

Both the multi-column script and the playscript take up about the same amount of space. The playscript is somewhat easier to handle on a word processor.

Both examples present a 3-way branch from the main menu. Clearly, the designer must be concerned with the control structure implied by the dialogue. No endless loops should be created: every path taken should eventually end up back at the START label.

In designing the control structure of a dialogue, it is worth remembering the constructs of structured programming. Every procedure - not just every computer program - can be built out of combinations of 3 building blocks:

- a single-entry, single-exit sequence of operations

- a single-entry, single-exit loop or repetition structure

- an IF-THEN-ELSE decision structure.

If you are in doubt about the clarity of the control structure of a dialogue, it is a good idea to step back from the detail and restructure the dialogue using the structures above. The technique of action diagramming is a help in doing this.

10.3   Action diagrams and Structured English

Structured English is a limited subset of English for describing procedures, consisting of:

- imperative sentences starting with action verbs (for example, "Multiply quantity by unit price")

- no undefined adjectives

- labels and/or logical connectors and/or conditions to show the structure.

Some examples are given in the following pages: for more details, see Ref. 10-1.

Sequence block

A single-entry single-exit block composed of a non-branching series of operations is shown like this:

```
|--[NAME]                              --|    [Input(s)]
|                                        |
|   Action A                             |
|                                        |
|   Action B                             |
|                                        |
|   Action C                           --|
|--                                      |    [Output(s)]
```

The start and end of the block is shown by the vertical bracket at the left. If the block is to be referred to by name, the name should be placed as shown. If you know the inputs and outputs for the block, you may optionally show them outside a vertical bracket at the right of the block.

For example, a block named "Compute hypotenuse of right triangle" may be shown like this:

```
|--Compute hypotenuse of right triangle--|      lengths of 2
|                                        |      shorter sides
|   Square length of Side 1              |
|   Square length of Side 2              |
|   Add squares together                 |
|   Take square root of sum              |
|--                                    --|      length of
                                               hypotenuse
```

Loop block

A loop block is denoted by a double line at the start. It may be given a name, but must always have the condition which specifies when the loop should terminate.

This may be in the form "For all ...." or "DO WHILE some condition is true."

```
|==[NAME]   Loop condition              --|      [Input(s)]
|                                        |
|   Action D                             |
|                                        |
|   Action E                             |
|                                        |
|   Action F                             |
|                                        |
|--[END LOOP]                           --|      [Output(s)]
```

As with a sequence block, if the inputs and outputs for the loop are known, they may be listed at the right. As an example:

```
|==IDENTIFY REORDER CANDIDATES.  For all products:
|
|   Retrieve quantity in stock now.
|
|   Compute average sales per day over last 7 days.
|
|   Compute how many days stock will last.
|
|   Compare with longest quoted delivery from any supplier.
|
|--END LOOP
```

Decision block

Decision blocks are of two kinds: the binary IF-ELSE structure in which one of two possibilities must apply, and the CASE structure in which several mutually exclusive possibilities are tested for, only one of which can apply.

The binary IF-ELSE is shown thus:

```
|--IF condition
|
|   Action P
|
|   Action Q
|
|--ELSE (not-condition)
|
|   Action R
|
|   Action S
|
|--[END IF]
```

It is good practice to spell out the situation that would cause the "ELSE" branch to be taken; that way the Structured English is more readable.

The CASE structure is shown like this:

```
|--IF condition A
|
|--ELSE IF condition B
|
|--ELSE IF condition C
|
|--ELSE (none of the above)
```

(Of course, the CASE structure can be reduced to binary IF-ELSEs in theory: in practice it makes more sense to display the alternatives as shown.)

You should always remember, and deal with, the possibility of the dangling ELSE at the end of the block; the situation that will arise if none of the mutually exclusive conditions apply. For example:

```
|--IF person is under 21
|     Covered under policy of parent
|
|--ELSE IF person is 21 - 35 inclusive
|     Premium is $150 per $1,000
|
|--ELSE IF person is 36 - 65 inclusive
|     Premium is $100 per $1,000
|
|--ELSE (person is over 65)
      Policy is not available
```

Abnormal exit

In some blocks, a condition may arise that makes continued normal processing impossible. Control needs to go directly to the exit of the block. Such a situation may be shown like this:

```
|--ROUTINE
|
|   Action A
|
|   Action B
|
|<-IF out-of-range  GO TO END ROUTINE
|
|   Action C
|
|   Action D
|
|--END ROUTINE
```

Note that a GO TO which moves control forward to an exit is not a violation of structured programming principles, because the block still has only one exit.

In practice, the various kinds of blocks are nested together. Consider the procedure which we began to lay out in the earlier dialogue.

If the caller is interested in a certain book, the operator has to enter whatever information the caller provides: the title, if the caller knows it, and/or the author's name, and/or any words indicating the title or the subject. The system will then search for all books in the database that match those criteria. If nothing is retrieved, presumably the caller is asking about a book which either is so new that it is not in the database yet, or is out of print. The operator should enter whatever details the caller can provide, promise that the book buyer (who knows the field) will research the title and get back to him or her, and ask what other books the caller is interested in.

If the details of the book are retrieved, the operator should give the caller the price and delivery time (displayed on the screen), and if the caller wants to order, enter the quantity, and how the caller wants the book(s) shipped (book rate, UPS, etc.). If the caller doesn't want to order this book, the operator should ask if he's interested in any other book.

This procedure could be represented by an action diagram thus:

```
|==For each book customer is interested in
|
|   Enter title or author name or key word
|
|   Search for matching titles
|
|   |--IF no hit
|   |
|   |   Enter whatever information customer has
|   |   Promise you'll research the book and get back to him
|<-|--Go on to next book
|   |
|   |--ELSE (book details retrieved)
|   |
|   |   Quote customer price and delivery time
|   |
|   |   |--IF customer wants to order
|   |   |     Enter quantity and shipment method
|   |   |
|   |   |--ELSE (doesn't want this book)
|   |   |     Ask if he's interested in any other book
|   |   |--ENDIF
|   |
|   |--ENDIF
|
|--END LOOP
```

This structure might itself be nested within a more comprehensive structure covering the whole order processing dialogue:

```
|--ORDER ROUTINE
|
|   Get customer phone number and enter
|
|   Retrieve cust record - display at bottom of screen
|                                           if available
|   |==For each book customer is interested in
|   |
|   |   Enter title or author name or key word
|   |
|   |   Search for matching titles
|   |
|   |   |--IF no hit
|   |   |
|   |   |   Enter whatever information customer has
|   |   |   Promise to research the book and get back to him
|<-|   |--Go on to next book
|   |   |
|   |   |--ELSE (book details retrieved)
|   |   |
|   |   |   Quote customer price and delivery time
|   |   |
|   |   |   |--IF customer wants to order
|   |   |   |    Enter quantity and shipment method
|   |   |   |
|   |   |   |--ELSE (doesn't want this book)
|   |   |   |    Ask if he's interested in any other book
|   |   |   |--ENDIF
|   |   |
|   |   |--ENDIF
|   |
|   |--END LOOP
|
|   |--IF customer has ordered anything
|   |
|   |   Enter shipping address/confirm if already retrieved
|   |   Enter billing address if different
|   |
|   |--ELSE (just an inquiry)
|   |
|   |   |--IF cust wants to be on mailing list
|   |   |
|   |   |   Enter/confirm address
|   |   |
|   |   |--ELSE (no interest)
|   |   |
|   |   |   Delete if displayed
|   |   |
|   |   |--ENDIF
|   |
|   |--ENDIF
|
|   Thanks for calling
|-- END ROUTINE
```

Once the dialogue is in this form, you can be confident that it has clean logic, with all logical possibilities considered, and without "spaghetti" control flows. The action diagram can either be used as the basis for prototyping and/or code generation, or it can be converted to one of the dialogue script formats, giving the operator detailed instructions as to what to say and do.

For more information on action diagrams, see Ref. 10-2.

References:

10-1 Gane, C. and Sarson, T. *Structured Systems Analysis: tools and techniques.* Englewood Cliffs, NJ: Prentice-Hall, 1979

10-2 Martin and McClure, *Action Diagrams: clearly structured program design.* Englewood Cliffs, NJ: Prentice-Hall, 1985

Exercises and discussion points:

1. Take a data entry dialogue with which you are familiar, which involves a conversation between the operator and another person.

    1.1 Produce a 5-column script to represent the dialogue.

    1.2 Convert the 5-column script to a play script.

    1.3 Draw an action diagram to show the logic structures of the dialogue.

2. Why must undefined adjectives (for example, "good" customer) be banned from Structured English?

3. What problems have you experienced with "over-the-wall" implementation? If you were responsible for receiving and implementing a specification for a procedure unit, what level of detail would you want it to contain, assuming you could have no contact with the analysts or users?

Chapter 11

"Fourth-generation" implementation languages

In Chapter 1, we noted that the term "fourth-generation language" (4GL) has come to be loosely applied to languages which are less procedural than COBOL. In general terms, the language which needs the fewest keystrokes or mouse-movements to get the application implemented is the highest-level and most productive language (provided that its source code is readable).

We also noted that a "full-feature" 4GL should include:

- a screen painter with access to a data dictionary

- a standard questionnaire for describing screen fields

- a default screen-application generator

- the ability to customize the default generator's output, especially by including SQL statements.

As an example of the type of facility available, we shall review the ORACLE Corporation's product, SQL*FORMS, which offers a version of the four facilities named above.

11.1 The SQL*FORMS default application generator

Suppose you have created, in a database managed by the ORACLE relational database manager, the PRODUCTS table which we used in Chapter 7. You have done this by issuing the CREATE TABLE statement:

CREATE TABLE PRODUCTS	. . .	The name you are giving the table is "PRODUCTS"
(CODE CHAR(4) NOT NULL,	. . .	Since CODE is the key identifier, you don't want it
		ever to be missing: defining it as NOT NULL
		means that a value must be provided for every row.
ITEM CHAR(12),	. . .	Note each column and datatype is separated by a comma
DESCRIPTION CHAR(15),		
PRICE NUMBER(5,2));	. . .	This means 5 positions in all, with 2 decimal places

The table exists, but is empty; you have not inserted any data into it.

What you would like to do is to write a program which would allow you to insert product data through the screen, to change the PRODUCTS table, and to query the table without writing lengthy SELECT statements. How long would you expect it would take you to write such a program? With SQL*FORMS it can be done in about one minute.

Once a table like PRODUCTS has been created, you can load the SQL*FORMS software and say you want to create a new application, which you will call, say, PRICING. You then will be shown a menu from which you can choose to create a custom screen, or set up a default screen.

If you choose the default screen, you will be asked to supply the table name (PRODUCTS in this case), and asked to say how many rows you would like to see on the screen at any one time.

You can choose which columns from PRODUCTS you want to see displayed; if you take the default, they will all appear on the screen. You now return to the main menu and select the GENERATE option; SQL*FORMS goes to work and using built-in rules, writes a program which will allow you to maintain and query the PRODUCTS table.

After a few seconds processing, SQL*FORMS responds:

```
Creation of application PRICING completed
```

and displays its main menu. To run PRICING you select the "RUN" option and enter the name PRICING.

You will then be shown a screen that SQL*FORMS has generated using its built-in logic, like this:

```
                        ========  PRODUCTS  ========

CODE      ITEM          DESCRIPTION        PRICE
```

You'll note that SQL*FORMS has used the table name as the header for the screen, and has the column names which you gave in the CREATE TABLE statement as the column headings (which are stored in the data dictionary), allowing two spaces between each field. If the total of the column widths had been such that they would not all fit on one line, SQL*FORMS would have defaulted to displaying just one record on the screen, with two fields per line.

As well as doing this simple-minded screen layout for you (note that SQL*FORMS is not smart enough to space the 4 columns across the screen, but crams them to the left), it has generated (without you seeing it) all the logic needed to insert, change, and query data in the PRODUCTS table.

If you enter the details of several products on the screen, (using function keys to go from column to column, and from row to row), and then press the COMMIT key ("End" on a PC keyboard), this automatically generated code will create an INSERT statement for each row.

If you then press the Enter Query key (F1 on the PC: each terminal has a different set of function key assignments), tab across to the ITEM column and enter Pliers, you are setting up a query which is the same as entering:

SELECT * FROM PRODUCTS WHERE ITEM = ' Pliers ' ;

When you press the Execute Query key (F2 on the PC), the application will retrieve and display the rows that meet the implied conditions you have set up, thus:

```
                            ========  PRODUCTS  ========

    CODE     ITEM          DESCRIPTION      PRICE

    T177     Pliers        Long nose        8.19
    T179     Pliers        Electrical       9.95
```

If you press Enter Query again, the data area will be blanked out, allowing a new query to be entered. You can enter combinations of conditions by, for example, entering Paintbrush under ITEM, and >3 under PRICE. This will produce a display of the paintbrushes selling for more than $3; the same as would have been produced by entering the query:

SELECT * FROM PRODUCTS WHERE ITEM = ' Paintbrush ' AND PRICE > 3

If you press Enter Query and then Execute Query without entering any conditions, you will get a listing of the whole table.

To update, for example, the price of a product, you first execute a query to get that product's row on the screen, then simply move the cursor to the entry, type in the new price, and then press the Commit key to commit the new value to the database.

So with a couple of dozen keystrokes, you have generated an application which carries out routine maintenance on the PRODUCTS table. The whole process takes a minute or two (once the table is created, which might take another minute).

The logic of the default application which is created for you can be summed up in this action diagram:

```
Select RUN option from main menu

|--IF you want to INSERT data into the table
|    Press "Create New Record" key (See map for your key board)
|    Enter values for each column (Press "Next Field" key
|       to go from column to column
|    (Press Down Arrow to enter a new record)
|    Press "Commit" key to insert record(s) into database
|
|   ELSE  IF you want to QUERY the table
|    Press "Enter Query" key
|    Enter values (with or without comparison operators)
|       in each relevant column
|    Press "Execute Query" key
|    IF query returns no records,  press "Abort Query" key
|
|   ELSE  IF you want to UPDATE the table
|    Enter a query (as above) to display the records that
|       need to be updated
|    Use the "Next Field" key and Up/Down arrows to put the
|       cursor on each value to be changed
|    Type in the new value
|    Press "Commit" key to change the record(s) in the database
|
|--ELSE (you want to DELETE data from the table)
|
|--END CASE
```

Of course, this application is quite crude: you may not like the default screen layout, or the screen heading, or the column headings. If you want to change them, this can be done quickly with the screen painter facility.

11.2 The SQL*FORMS screen painter

To use the screen painter, you choose MODIFY from the main menu, and name the "form" you want to work on, in this case PRICING. The screen is displayed; you can change any of the headings by moving the cursor to the one you want to change, and typing in the new heading.

You can draw a box round any area on the screen by selecting the points where you want the upper left and lower right corners of the box to be, and pressing the "Make a Box" function key. (If the two corners are on the same horizontal or vertical line, you'll get a box which is collapsed to a single line.)

To move a field (perhaps you want to center the four fields on the screen), you place the cursor on the field, press the Select key, move the cursor to the new position, and press the Move key.

To add a new field (maybe Quantity in Stock), you move the cursor to the place where the field is to start, press Select, then move to the place where the field is to end, and press Select again. Then you press the Create Field key. SQL*FORMS will then display a "pop-up" area on the screen like this:

```
 ------------------------------------------------
|        DEFINE FIELD            Seq # ---       |
|                                                |
| Name ----------------------------------------- |
| Data type:                                     |
|   CHAR     NUMBER      RNUMBER      DATE        |
|   ALPHA    INT         RINT         JDATE       |
|            MONEY       RMONEY       EDATE       |
| Actions:                                       |
|   SQL      ATTRIBUTES       VALIDATION          |
 ------------------------------------------------
```

You enter the sequence # for the new field (5 in this case if it is to be to the right of the existing 4 fields), and enter its name. Then you select the data type from the options presented (several of which are specific to ORACLE). In this case you would select RINT to get a right-justified integer field.

If you now put the cursor on ATTRIBUTES, SQL*FORMS will display another pop-up like the one on the following page:

```
 _____
|                      |
| SPECIFY ATTRIBUTES   |
|   Database Field     | - field on screen corresponds to a field in database
|   Primary Key        | - this field is (part of) the primary key of the table
|                      |
|   Displayed          | - the field will appear on the screen (fields can be defined but invisible)
|   Input allowed      | - you can enter data with this field
|   Update allowed     | - you can change data retrieved into this field by a query
|   Fixed length       | - the value you enter must be exactly as long as the field
|   Mandatory          | - the field cannot be left blank
|   Uppercase          | - lower case letters will be converted on entry
|   Autoskip           | - when a fixed length field is full,
|                      |   the cursor will jump to the next field
|_____|
```

You select the options that apply to the Quantity In Stock field. In this case it will be a field in the database (you should alter the table to add an IN_STOCK_QTY column), but will not be the primary key. It will be displayed; you want to be able to enter values and to change values if they are not correct. It cannot be fixed length, and should probably be made mandatory (if you enter a new product, you should enter the quantity in stock, even if it's zero). "Uppercase" and "autoskip" are irrelevant for this field.

When you have selected the attributes that should apply, you press the Accept key to store your choices, and SQL*FORMS will display the DEFINE FIELD pop-up again. From this, you should next select the VALIDATION action, which will show a pop-up like this:

```
 _____
|                                   |
|       SPECIFY VALIDATION          |
| Field Length 4_   Query Length __ | - specify if different from the length selected
| KEY Block _____        |
| COPY Fld  _____        | - if the field value can be copied from elsewhere
| DEFAULT   _____        | - if you want a standard (changeable)
| RANGE Low _____        |   default value to be displayed
|      High _____        | - for editing
| LIST  Tab _____        | -} if a list of values can be found in some table
|    Column _____        | }
| HELP:                             |
| Enter value for: IN_STOCK QTY     | - the message the operator will see if
|_____|   he presses the Help key.
                                         This is the default message, but you
                                         can supply any 80 character message you
                                         want, and optionally have it automatically
                                         displayed at the bottom of the screen
                                         whenever the cursor enters the field, thus
                                         giving the operator quite detailed prompts.
```

This pop-up enables you to specify how the field should be edited, plus some other characteristics. In this case, there is no relevant DEFAULT that should be placed in the field every time the screen is displayed: DEFAULT is useful when, for example, 98% of all transactions are for cash, so that a default value of "Cash" in the HOW_PAID field would need to be over-ridden only 2% of the time.

If you specify a RANGE, then values outside that range will be rejected.

Once the VALIDATION options have been selected, you press the Accept key to return to the DEFINE FIELD pop-up.

Lastly, you could select the SQL action to enter a SQL statement that would be executed when this field was changed. For example, if you wanted to have the ITEM, DESCRIPTION and PRICE displayed whenever you entered a product code (without pressing any query keys), you would attach to the CODE field the statement:

```
SELECT ITEM, DESCRIPTION, PRICE
   INTO ITEM, DESCRIPTION, PRICE      (field names in an INTO clause refer to screen fields)
      FROM PRODUCTS
         WHERE CODE = &CODE           (&CODE means "the value of the CODE field
                                        entered on the screen")
```

In the case of IN_STOCK_QTY, no SQL statement is relevant, so you press Accept again, and are returned to the screen painter with all your choices for the new field stored in the database, along with the modified screen definition.

(For more details of the field definition options, see Ref. 11-1.)

If you wanted to create a completely custom screen from scratch, of course, you would follow a similar procedure for all the fields on the screen. The screen painter also enables you to draw boxes and lines, to improve the clarity of the display.

11.3   Where's the source code?

SQL*FORMS has many more facilities than have been mentioned in this brief review. As well as attaching SQL statements to fields, as we just discussed, fields can be grouped into blocks (areas of the screen each accessing a different table) and SQL statements can be triggered when a block is used for a query, insert, update, or delete.   IF statements can be attached to fields or blocks to allow branching logic (with its attendant debugging problems!).

SQL*FORMS is not the only such rapid application generation facility. Relational Technology Inc. markets a very comparable product, Applications-By-Forms (ABF) for use with their INGRES relational DBMS.

At the time of writing, there seems to be no language of comparable power available for users of DB2.

Both SQL*FORMS and ABF can be described as "visual programming" tools. The specification of screen display and processing is done while looking at the resultant screen itself, not by changing source code, compiling, running, and then seeing the consequences of the source code changes.   This is a powerful aid to rapid development.

Both SQL*FORMS and ABF store the "source code" - the field locations, options, and SQL statements - in tables in the relational databases (ORACLE and INGRES respectively).   These tables can be listed out if required, and can be put into a text file format for detailed editing.

SQL*FORMS presents such a text file in the form of a series of prompts to which you, the application designer, can respond appropriately.   When you use the screen painter, and the definition pop-ups, you are supplying the responses to those prompts.

When you select the default generation option, SQL*FORMS will use its best intelligence to supply its own answers to the prompts (for example, to establish where on the screen the various columns should appear).

The listing starting on the next page shows an extract from the PRICING "source code" listing of prompts and responses, with some explanatory comments.

(SQL*FORMS is abbreviated to S*F)

STANDARD PROMPTS FROM SQL*FORMS	RESPONSES SUPPLIED BY YOU OR GENERATED BY DEFAULT	COMMENTS
;Application Title:	PRICING	*S*F uses the name you supplied.*
;ORACLE workspace size:	10/1	*S*F assigns 10K bytes.*
;Block name / Description:	PRODUCTS12	*Each table (in this case there is only one) is handled by a block of fields on the screen. S*F assigns a block name composed of the table-name plus 2 arbitrary digits.*
;Table name:	PRODUCTS	*S*F uses the table name that you supplied.*
;Check for uniqueness before inserting Y/N:	N	*One can specify that the key field(s) of a new row should be checked for uniqueness before insertion in the table. S*F doesn't bother.*
;Display/Buffer how many records:	15/30	*You specified that the 15 records would be displayed on the screen. S*F keeps up to twice that number in a memory buffer for faster access should they be required.*
;Base crt line?	5	*This specifies that the first row of the 15 possible rows will appear on line 5 of the screen.*
;How many physical lines per record?	1	*S*F allows 1 physical screen line per record, since it calculates from the lengths of the columns in the table that they will all fit on one line.*

/continued

174

The responses on this page specify the first field in the block:

```
;Field name:                    CODE }
;Type of field:                 CHAR }   S*F gets this information from
;Length of field:                  4 }   the table definition.
;Is this field in the base table: Y }
```

```
;Is this field part of
    the primary key Y/N::              Y
```
*S*F assumes that the first field in the table is the primary key i.e. uniquely identifies each row.   It follows that if you plan to use S*F, you should put the primary key first in the table.*

```
;Field to copy primary key from:
```
*This question only applies when there are other blocks in the application, so S*F ignores it.*

```
;Default value:
```
*One can supply a default value that the operator can override if appropriate; S*F does not do so.*

```
;Page:                             1 }   S*F will start this field  in the first
;Line:                             1 }   column of  the  first line (in fact
;Column:                           1 }   line 5) of the first (and in this case
                                         the only) screen page.
```

```
;Prompt:                        CODE
```
*S*F uses the field name as a column heading.*

```
;Display prompt above field:       Y
```
Otherwise, it will be at the left of the field.

```
;Display prompt once for block:    Y
```
At the top of the screen, not on every line.

```
;Allow field to be entered Y/N:    Y
```
If N, a value may be displayed but it cannot be changed, i.e. nothing new can be keyed into the field.

```
;SQL>
```
This is where SQL statement(s) would be entered if relevant. This simple application requires none.

```
;Is field fixed length Y/N:        N
```
*If a field is fixed length, S*F will only accept entries of that exact length.*

/continued

```
;Auto jump to next field Y/N:        N
```
If you specify Auto Jump, the cursor will move on to the next field as soon as the field has been filled, which saves pressing the TAB key.

```
;Convert field to upper case:        N
```
If Y, letters entered are converted to capitals which avoids having to remember to press the Shift key. S*F does not do this.

```
;Help message:     Enter value for:      CODE
```
S*F provides this message which will be displayed at the bottom of the screen if the operator presses the Help key.

```
;Lowest value:                       }
```
If relevant, you can specify the lowest and

```
;Highest value:                      }
```
highest values that should be accepted by S*F. The default is to ignore these.

The following responses specify the second field in the block.

The comments on them are the same as for CODE, with the differences below:

```
;Field name:                     ITEM
;Type of field:                  CHAR
;Length of field:                12
;Is this field in the base table: Y

;Is this field part of
    the primary key Y/N:         N
```
Since this is not the first field, S*F assumes it is not part of the key.

(Note that the question asked for CODE about copying the primary key is not relevant here.)

```
;Default value:

;Page:                           1
;Line:                           1
```

/continued

```
;Column:                              8        S*F works out a column to start
                                               the field in,  based on the widths
                                               of all the fields in the table.

;Prompt:                             ITEM
;Display prompt above field:          Y
;Display prompt once for block:       Y

;Allow field to be entered Y/N:       Y
;Allow field to be updated Y/N:       Y        S*F assumes that all non-key
                                               fields should be capable of being
                                               updated.  Note that this question
                                               was not asked for CODE because
                                               a key field once given a value
                                               uniquely identifying the record,
                                               should not normally be changed.

;SQL>

;Is field mandatory Y/N:              N        If you specify that a field is
                                               mandatory, IAP will not allow the
                                               operator to go on without entering
                                               a value.  Note again that this was
                                               not asked of CODE because a
                                               key field is mandatory by
                                               definition.

;Is field fixed length Y/N:          N

;Auto jump to next field Y/N:        N

;Convert field to upper case:        N

;Help message:    Enter value for:   ITEM

;Lowest value:

;Highest value:
```

The following responses specify the third field in the block.

```
;Field name:                         DESCRIPTION
;Type of field:                      CHAR
;Length of field:                    15
;Is this field in the base table:    Y

;Is this field part of
    the primary key Y/N::            N
```

/continued

```
;Default value:
;Page:                                     1
;Line:                                     1

;Column:                                  23    As with ITEM, S*F works out a
                                                column to start the field in, based
                                                on the widths of all the fields in
                                                the table.
```

The other prompts about the field are handled for DESCRIPTION and for PRICE in a precisely comparable way to the responses for ITEM, then:

```
;Field name:                             <R>    When no more fields remain to be
                                                specified,      S*F supplies a
                                                <Return> for the next field name.


;Block name / Description:               <R>    Since there are no more fields in
                                                the first block,  this question is
                                                asked to prompt for another
                                                block.   Since there is no other
                                                block,   S*F supplies another
                                                <Return>.


;Enter text for form                            The last question asks for any
                                                fixed text or graphics needed to
                                                make up the form which will
                                                appear on the screen.
                              %LINE
                                2               S*F simply puts on line 2 of the
                                                screen ...


              ======== PRODUCTS ========        . . . a heading composed of the
                                                      table name
                              %END              . . . and signs off.
```

Source code is less important with a visual programming tool than with a conventional language. If you want to change a screen layout, don't go to the source code, instead bring up the screen in question, and use the screen painter. If you want to change a SQL statement, go to the field in question, invoke the SQL action in the DEFINE field pop-up and change the SQL statement displayed. Generally speaking, you only need to see a listing if there is a series of SQL statements associated with a field or a block, and you want to think through what will happen as each is executed.

11.4 Full-feature 4GLs, prototyping and top-down implementation

With a "visual programming" implementation language of the power of SQL*FORMS or ABF, the whole concept of prototyping undergoes a change. A screen layout produced in 5 minutes with the default generator and screen painter is more than just a prototype; it has update and query logic already built into it, it interacts with the real database, and generates a version of the final executable code. It makes more sense to regard it as a "skeleton" of the complete procedure-unit, to which more functionality can be added, rather than as a demonstration of the system which will be thrown away once the "real" code is developed.

This dovetails neatly with the "top-down" approach to implementation discussed in Chapter 1. A skeleton version of the complete system can be produced using SQL*FORMS for the interactive PUs, and simple SQL statements for the batch PUs. Once the skeleton has been tested and shown to accept input, update the database correctly, and generate output with the correct content, if not the correct format, a second version of the system can be planned which has more error checking functions, more computation, and better formatted output. Once the second version has been tested and shown to function correctly, later versions can be implemented and tested, until the full system is delivered.

As an example, consider how this approach might be applied to the system which we discussed in the overview of Chapter 1. From the "physicalized" data flow diagram, we defined 9 procedure units in all, as shown on the next page.

First, of course, each table must be defined and created in the database. Then the tables which describe objects (PRODUCTS, SUPPLIERS, PRODUCT_SOURCES) must be populated with some realistic test data. A default SQL*FORMS application could be generated for each table, and used to create, say 2 products, and 2 suppliers; a prototype or skeleton of PUs 6 and 7 would thus be developed.

For PU 1 ("Process orders"), a default interactive application could be created accessing both the SALES and SALE_ITEMS table from the same screen. In the default version, the user would enter the salesperson's initials, the SALE_NO, and the date in the upper part of the screen, and for each item sold, enter the sale number, the code, the quantity sold, and the item charge, in the lower part of the screen.

ID	DFD name	Tables accessed
1	Process orders	PRODUCTS, SALES, SALE_ITEMS
2	Prepare bank deposits	SALES, SALE_ITEMS
3	Sales reports	SALES, SALE_ITEMS
4-1	Determine products that need ordering	PRODUCTS, SALES, SALE_ITEMS
4-2	Select best supplier	SUPPLIERS, PRODUCT_SOURCES PURCHASE_ORDERS, DELIVERIES
4-3	Confirm PO	SUPPLIERS, PRODUCT_SOURCES PURCHASE_ORDERS
5	Analyze shipment	PURCHASE_ORDERS, DELIVERIES
6	Maintain PRODUCTS	PRODUCTS
7	Maintain SUPPLIERS/ PRODUCT_SOURCES	SUPPLIERS, PRODUCT_SOURCES

Once the version is working, the default version would be modified to automatically increment the SALE_NO, and copy the current value into each sale item record, and to use the system date as the sale date, unless the user wanted to override it. In the sale-items part of the screen, a SQL statement would be added to the CODE field which would retrieve and display the product's name when a code was entered. Likewise, a SQL statement would be added to the QTY_SOLD field which would retrieve the SALE_PRICE from the PRODUCTS table, and compute and display the ITEM_CHARGE.

This skeleton could then be exercised with representative users, who could give feedback on the screen layout, and the prompts and help messages. They might ask, for example, to see the time of day displayed on the screen, as well as the date. They might ask to see a message displayed when the quantity in stock falls below a certain number, and so on.

Once some sales have been captured (albeit only for the two PRODUCTS in the tables so far), a skeleton batch SQL routine could be written to produce the raw data for the bank deposit documents, and to produce an unformatted sales report. Provided all the data needed has been captured, format statements can then be added to produce these outputs in exactly the layout required.

Similar approaches would be taken with each of the other procedure units.

Reference

11-1   Gane, C.   *Developing Business Systems in SQL using ORACLE on the IBM PC*.   New York: Rapid System Development Inc., 1986

Information about SQL*FORMS is available from:

> ORACLE Corporation
> 20 Davis Drive
> Belmont, CA 94002
> 800/345-DBMS

Information about APPLICATIONS-BY-FORMS is available from:

> Relational Technology Inc.
> 1080 Marina Village Parkway
> Alameda, CA 94501
> 415/769-1400

Exercises and discussion points:

1.   If written in your favorite language, how many keystrokes would it take you to implement the "default" file maintenance/query application described in this chapter?

2.   Review some interactive applications with which you are familiar. What proportion of them could be implemented with the basic subset of SQL*FORMS presented in this chapter?   What extra screen or data manipulation commands would you need?

Appendix A

CASE tools

As the value of logical modelling has become more widely recognized, and as powerful personal computers have become widely available, a number of vendors have developed packages which enable logical models to be developed and stored in machine-readable form, so that they can be easily changed and printed out. The first such tool was STRADIS/DRAW, which was marketed by McDonnell Douglas in 1982. This used a Tektronix workstation to build up data flow diagrams, storing them on a mainframe computer. In 1984, Index Technology (Intech) introduced EXCELERATOR, which runs on a stand-alone 512 Mb PC/XT or larger machine, and enables the user to create and modify data flow diagrams, entity-relationship diagrams, structure charts and other modelling diagrams. Further, it enables the user to build up a design database on the PC hard disk, describing all objects and connections on all diagrams, and holding the definitions of all data elements and data structures. This data dictionary can be accessed by EXCELERATOR's screen/report prototyping aid.

EXCELERATOR has been widely accepted, with over 10,000 copies shipped at the time of writing. Many other products have been introduced offering broadly similar capabilities. These products have become referred to as Computer-Aided Software Engineering (CASE) tools.

Broadly speaking, CASE tools contain some or all of these six software components:

1. a graphics front-end, which enables the user to build up diagrams of various kinds on the screen of the workstation (usually a large PC). Some CASE tools can only handle data flow diagrams, some can produce a wide range of graphics.

2. a data catalog or repository which enables descriptions of all the data elements, data stores, entities, processes, and so on to be stored in an integrated manner. The package may or may not have an interface to the corporate data dictionary on the mainframe. The package may or may not support formal process logic such as action diagrams.

3.   a prototyping aid for automated development of screen and report layouts.

4.   a code-generation/database-definition facility for generating all or part of executable programs in a target language(s) from the process specification logic, and generating physical database definitions in various DBMSs from the data dictionary.

5.   a reverse-engineering facility for extracting logical models and process specification logic from physical database definitions and source code.

6.   a documentation generation facility for producing requirements documentation, program specifications, and other documents using the contents of the data dictionary, and including diagrams from the logical model.   Many CASE tools provide standard interfaces to popular desktop-publishing packages.

In evaluating any CASE tool, one should ask which of these 6 facilities it offers, and for each facility one should investigate the exact capabilities available.

The degree of integration between the various facilities is also important, obviously. For instance, the prototyping aid should be able to access the data definitions stored in the data repository; the code-generation capability should be able to use the screen layouts developed with the prototyping aid, and so on.

This is a fast-growing area and one with great potential for speeding up system development along the lines presented in this book.

Some vendors of CASE tools:

Bachman Information Systems Inc. (BACHMAN Product Set)
Four Cambridge Center
Cambridge, MA 02142
617/354-1414

CADRE Technologies (TEAMWORK)
222 Richmond Street
Providence, RI 02903
401/351-5951

Index Technology (EXCELERATOR)
1 Main Street
Cambridge, MA 02142
617/494-8200

Interactive Development Environments (Software through Pictures)
595 Market Street, Ste. 1200
San Francisco, CA 94105
415/543-0900

LBMS (AUTO-MATE PLUS)
2900 North Loop West, Ste. 800
Houston, TX 77092
713/682-8530 or 800/231-7515

Knowledgeware (Information Engineering Workbench)
3340 Peachtree Road NE
Atlanta, GA 30026
404/231-8575

McDonnell Douglas ISG (ProKit Workbench)
P.O. Box 516/L863
St. Louis, MO 63166
314/232-5715

Nastec Corp. (Design Aid)
24681 Northwestern Highway
Southfield, MI 48075
313/353-3300

Texas Instruments (Information Engineering Facility)
PO Box 869305, Drawer 8474
Plano, TX 75086
214/575-4404

Glossary

ABF

See Applications-By-Forms

Action diagram

A technique for representing procedure logic with blocks of Structured English or pseudocode, delimited by horizontal and vertical lines.

Active data dictionary

A data dictionary which holds physical data definitions and locations, and which can be accessed at execution time, so that no data definitions are needed in the executable programs.

Alias

See Synonym

Applications-By-Forms

The application generator facility integrated with **INGRES**.

Arbitrary key

A primary key which is added to a table, additional to the meaningful data stored in the table, having the sole purpose of ensuring that each row can be uniquely identified by a single column. Usually the values of the arbitrary key are machine generated.

Attribute

A data element which holds information describing an entity.

Bottom-up implementation

The usual approach to coding and testing in which the programs making up a system are first coded and tested, and then integrated afterwards. Compare with **Top-down implementation**.

Business objective

An objective of a project which can be stated in terms of increased revenue, avoided cost, improved service, reduced risk, improved competitive position, greater market share or some other measure which directly impacts profitability. Compare with **System objective.**

Candidate key

An attribute or group of attributes whose value(s) uniquely identify each row in a table.

Cartesian product

The Cartesian product of two tables is a new table formed by taking each row in one table, and adding to it each row in the other table.

CASE structure

A single-entry, single-exit decision structure, specifically for handling several mutually exclusive but similar cases.

CASE tool

A software package for Computer-Aided Software Engineering.

Code interpretation table

A table with two columns, containing the values of a code in one column, and the meaning of each value in the other.

Cold-turkey approach

(to modelling an existing system whose internals are not understood.) Examination of the outputs from a system to deduce from the outputs the data that must be stored in the system's files, followed by examination of the inputs to see how they correspond to the stored data. Compare with **Grease-monkey approach.**

Continuous (data element or domain)

One which can take up so many values that it is not practical to list them; normally an eligible value is one which satisfies some rule. See also **Discrete**.

Current logical system (model)

The underlying essence of an existing system represented by its data flow diagram, entity-relationship diagram, stored data structures, and procedure logic expressed in a way which is as free as possible of the particular physical implementation.

Current physical system

The screens, input documents, reports, physical file structures, program code, user manuals and other documentation of some existing system.

Database Administrator

A person (or group) responsible for the control and integrity of one or more databases.

Database Management System

An integrated set of computer programs which allow multiple concurrent users to manipulate one or more shared databases, with provisions for controlled secure access, and for recovery of data in the case of machine or other failure.

Data Catalog

A store of data describing the data (and maybe the processes) in a logical system model.

Data Dictionary

One or more files or tables describing the nature, structure and location of the data in a database.

Data element

The smallest unit of data which is meaningful for the purpose. In a relational database, a data element is stored as a column in a table; it may appear on a screen or a report as a field, possibly in different formats.

Data Flow Diagram

A chart showing the flow of data in any information system, showing the sources/destinations of data outside the system, the processes which transform data and the places where data is stored.

Data model

An entity-relationship diagram plus a set of 4NF tables, one for each block on the diagram, with associated related tables, plus a definition of each data element in each table.

Data store

A location where data is stored between transactions or between executions of the system; in a relational database, a data store is equivalent to one or more (related) tables.

DBA

See **Database Administrator**

DBMS

See **Database Management System**

Degree marker

A conventional symbol added to the relationship or association line between two entities on an Entity-Relationship diagram to show whether there is one or many of the particular entity involved in the relationship.

DFD

See **Data Flow Diagram**

Discrete (data element or domain)

One which takes up only a limited number of values, each of which usually has a meaning. See also **Continuous.**

Discovery prototyping

An approach to requirements definition which encourages users to discover their needs by working with a rapidly generated prototype of all or part of the proposed system.

Domain

A set of eligible values which can be taken up by one or more data elements, defined by a rule or a list.

EEIO listing
> A list of External Entities for a system, with each Input that comes from any one of them, and each Output that goes to any one of them.

Embedded structures
> A data structure which is regarded as a single element by its users, but one or more parts of which has a special meaning.

Entity
1.   A data entity is something, usually having multiple attributes, about which data is held in an information system.

2.   An external entity is something outside an information system which is a source and/or destination of data to and/or from the system.

> Data entities may correspond to external entities, and vice versa, but not necessarily.

Entity-Relationship analysis
> The process of identifying significant data entities for a system and representing the associations between them as non-collapsible 1-to-1 relationships, or 1-to-many relationships.

E-R
> See **Entity-Relationship Analysis**

Executive Sponsor
> A senior business executive who assumes final responsibility for the success of an information system project.

Explosion
> Representation of the details of a process on a DFD by drawing another DFD, in which each process represents a part of the original process.

External Entity
> See **Entity**

Facilitator
> A participant in a meeting whose primary responsibility is to see that the meeting is conducted in the most productive manner.

Fifth Normal Form
> A fourth normal form relation also is in fifth normal form when its information content cannot be reconstructed from two or more smaller relations, not having the same key.

First Normal Form

      A relation with only one value in each cell, (i.e. no repeating groups) but which does not necessarily meet the test for higher normal forms.

Fission

      The process of replacing a complex process on a DFD with several simpler processes on the same DFD. Compare with **Explosion.**

FOCUS

      A 4GL marketed by Information Builders Inc.

Foreign key

      A column in a table which may or may not be (part of) the key of that table, but is (part of) the key in some other table.

Fourth generation language

      A computer language which is significantly less procedural than COBOL.

Fourth Normal Form

      A third normal form relation is also in fourth normal form if it does not contain more than one multi-valued fact about the entity described by the table.

Grease-monkey approach

      (to modelling an existing system whose internals are not understood.) Examination of the program code and physical file dumps, to understand the logical data structures and procedure logic of the system. Compare with **Cold-turkey approach.**

Group memory

      A term for the display of agendas, decisions, issues, products, etc., developed in the course of a group workshop.

GUIDE

      An organization of IBM users, with offices at 111 E. Wacker Drive, Chicago, IL.

Homonym

      (Webster, "One of two or more words spelled and pronounced alike but different in meaning"), specifically a data element name which stands for different data elements in different contexts.

ILGI

      See **Impartial-Leader Group Interview**

Impartial-Leader Group Interview (*JAD*)

      The replacement of conventional serial interviewing of the prospective users of an information system, by a workshop attended by all the users, facilitated by an impartial session leader.

Index

A data store that holds information about the physical location of stored records with certain attribute values, so that given an attribute value, the corresponding record(s) can be retrieved quickly.

INGRES

A relational DBMS marketed by Relational Technology Inc.

Integrity checker

A program which examines all the tables in a database, to see if there are any detectable mismatches or inconsistencies.

Interface bug

A system problem caused by an inability to send data across the interface between two parts of the system which are otherwise working properly (or between a part of the system and an external entity).

Intersection entity

A table which is created to describe the association between two other entities which have a many-to-many relationship with each other.

JAD

See **Joint Application Design**

Joint Application Design

The Impartial-Leader Group Interview technique developed and supported by IBM.

Join

1.   The process of combining two or more tables which share a common column.

2.   The combined table produced as a result of a join operation.

Key, foreign

See **Foreign key**

Key, primary

One (or a combination of) attribute(s), column(s) or field(s) which is chosen as the unique identifier of a row or record in a table or file.

Logical

1.   Conforming to the laws of logic.

2.   Representing the underlying nature or essence of something, particularly an information system.

MANTIS

A 4GL marketed by CINCOM Inc.

Multi-valued fact

A data element which may have more than one value for a single instance of an entity.

NATURAL

A 4GL marketed by Software A.G.

Non-procedural language

A computer language which enables the programmer to specify what should be done, rather than how the computer should carry it out.

Normalization

The procedure of taking a data structure and representing it as one or more 4NF tables.

ORACLE

A relational DBMS marketed by the ORACLE Corp.

Physical

To do with the particular way data or logic is represented or implemented in a given system at a given time.

Physicalized DFD

A DFD on which the processes correspond to physical procedure units, rather than to logical groupings.

Primary key

See **Key, primary**

Procedure unit

A grouping of automated and/or manual procedures which can be executed as a unit.

Process

A group of operations which transform data in some way.

Projection

The process of producing a new table by extracting certain columns from an existing table.

Prototyping

The production of a piece of software which superficially resembles a proposed system, more quickly and cheaply than a version of the system can be developed in the target language.

Pseudocode

A technique for specifying procedure or program logic in readable form without conforming to the syntax of any particular programming language.

PU

See **Procedure unit**

Realizing join

The creation of an actual table which has the same structure as a table produced by joining two or more other actual physical tables.

Referential integrity

If in every case where there should be a record in some table to match a record in another table, the matching record(s) do, in fact, exist, then the database has referential integrity.

Refinement prototyping

The detailed definition of screen and report formats by exercising prototypes with representative users and modifying them based on user feedback.

Relation

A two-dimensional table in which if the left-to-right order of columns were changed, or the sequence of rows were changed, no information would be lost.

Relational database

A database made up of relations.

Relationship description

On an Entity-Relationship diagram, the description of the type of association between two entities. For example, if each employee is assigned to a project, then "is assigned to" is the description of this relationship between employees and projects.

Repeating group

Two or more data elements, forming a group structure, which occur more than once for every instance of another related data structure.

RM

A conventional DFD symbol (short for "Routine Maintenance") placed at the upper right hand corner of a data store to signify that this data store will be subject to additions, changes, and deletions from at least one procedure unit which is not shown on the diagram.

Robert's rules of order

The standard rules for the conduct of parliamentary, committee, and other meetings.

Routine maintenance

The process of making additions to, changes to, and deletions from a data store representing some object, such as customers or employees.

Rubber-banding

If a graphics package has a rubber-banding facility, then when a graphics symbol connected to other symbols is moved on the screen, the connection lines are automatically adjusted to keep the same relative start and end points, as though each connection were a rubber band.

Screen painter

A generic term for a software facility which enables executable screen layout definitions to be built up by placing the cursor on various parts of the screen where literals/variables should appear, and issuing appropriate commands.

Scribe

The meeting participant(s) who are responsible for recording the proceedings and/or building up the group memory.

Search argument

The column(s) used as a basis for retrieving data from a data store, for example, the column(s) referred to in the ... WHERE ... clause of a SELECT statement.

Second Normal Form (2NF)

A 1NF relation in which all of the non-key columns are dependent on (can only be told by knowing) the whole of the key. (A 1NF relation with only one column as its key is automatically in 2NF).

Selection

The process of making a new table by extracting selected rows from another table.

Serial interviewing

The conventional approach to requirements definition in which each prospective user is interviewed separately by an analyst.

Session leader

See **Facilitator**

SQL

The normal abbreviation for Structured Query Language, a data definition, manipulation and control language developed by IBM, and adopted in 1986 as the American National Standard Database Language (X3.135).

SQL*FORMS

A full-feature 4GL integrated with the ORACLE relational DBMS.

SQL*PLUS

A superset of SQL for the handling of batch (set-processing) queries, integrated with the ORACLE relational DBMS.

Steering Body

The definition and review group for an information system development project, made up of those managers whose business areas will be impacted by the system (for well or for ill).

Structured English

A technique for representing business policies and procedures in a limited subset of English using single-entry, single-exit logic structures.

Sub-query

A SELECT statement nested within the ... WHERE ... clause of another SELECT statement.

Sub-type

An entity which represents a sub-class of the instances of another entity. For example, PREVIOUS_EMPLOYEES is a sub-type of EMPLOYEES.

Super-type

An entity which is generalized enough to comprehend two or more sub-types. For example, "Legislators" is a super-type for "Senators" and "Representatives."

Synonym

(Webster, "One of two or more words ... that have the same ... meaning ..."), specifically the name of a data element which is not the same as its principal name.

System objective

An objective for an information system which is stated in terms of capturing, storing, and/or delivering data faster, more accurately, more comprehensively, or more useably. Compare with **Business objective**.

Third Normal Form (3NF)

A 2NF relation is also in 3NF if no non-key column is dependent on (can be computed from) any other non-key column(s).

Top-down implementation

An approach to coding and testing in which a skeleton version of a system is produced first to test the interfaces between the parts of the system, and between the system and the outside world.

Tuple

A row in a table which represents a **relation.**

User Representative

1.   A supervisor/clerical person who knows the meaning of data and the detailed business policy and procedural rules which have to built into a system.

2.   Someone who is typical of the people who will use the screens and reports of a system in their work.

View

An apparent, or virtual, table; defined in the data dictionary in terms of columns in real "base" tables.

1NF

See **First Normal Form**

2NF

See **Second Normal Form**

3NF

See **Third Normal Form**

4GL

See **Fourth Generation Language**

4NF

See **Fourth Normal Form**

5NF

See **Fifth Normal Form**

Index